Imagine That! Picture This!

Collection for Readers

- 30 Very Easy Stories
- For Use with Intervention Handbook
- Take-Home Version in Blackline Master Form

Editorial Offices: Glenview, Illinois • Parsippany, New Jersey • New York, New York
Sales Offices: Parsippany, New Jersey • Duluth, Georgia • Glenview, Illinois
Carrollton, Texas • Ontario, California

Acknowledgments

Photography

Every effort has been made to secure permission and provide appropriate credit for photographic material. The publisher deeply regrets any omission and pledges to correct errors called to their attention in subsequent editions.

Unless otherwise acknowledged, all photographs are the property of Scott Foresman, a division of Pearson Education.

Reader 3, 1: David Young-Wolff/PhotoEdit; **3, 7:** © Bob Daemmrich/Daemmrich Photography; **5:** © Bob Daemmrich/Stock Boston; **Reader 5, 1:** Rich Pedroncelli/AP/Wide World; **2:** Manny Millan/SI/TimePix; **4:** John W. McDonough/SI/TimePix; **7:** Eric Draper/AP/Wide World; **8–9:** © AFP/Corbis; **10:** John W. McDonough/SI/TimePix; **Reader 6, 1:** © Jack Wilburn/Animals Animals/Earth Scenes; **3, 5:** © David Sieren/Visuals Unlimited; **7:** © Joe McDonald/Animals Animals/Earth Scenes; **Reader 8, 1:** © Pat Armstrong/Visuals Unlimited; **5:** Alan R. Moller/Stone; **6–7:** © Albert Copley/Visuals Unlimited; **Reader 9, 1:** © Brian Rogers/Visuals Unlimited; **3:** © Fritz Polking/Visuals Unlimited; **5:** © Gerald & Buff Cors/Visuals Unlimited; **7:** © Hugh S. Rose/Visuals Unlimited; **Reader 10, 1:** © Bob Krist/Corbis; **3:** © Johnny Johnson/ Animals Animals/Earth Scenes; **5:** Bruce McMillan; **7:** Stephen W. Kress/Stephen W. Kress; **9:** © Patti Murray/Animals Animals/Earth Scenes; **10:** © Richard Hamilton Smith/Corbis; **Reader 11, 1:** © Bill Aron/ PhotoEdit; **3:** © Tony Freeman/PhotoEdit; **5:** PhotoDisc; **7:** © Michael Newman/PhotoEdit; **Reader 13, 1:** © S. McBrady/PhotoEdit; **2:** Barbara Alper/Stock Boston; **4:** © Myrleen Ferguson/PhotoEdit; **7:** Charles Gupton/Stock Boston; **Reader 18, 1:** © Tony Freeman/PhotoEdit; **3:** Cameramann International, Ltd./Milt & Joan Mann/Cameramann International, Ltd.; **5:** Dave Baumhefner/ NOAA; **Reader 21, 1, 4:** Brown Brothers; **7:** Culver Pictures Inc.; **Reader 22, 2–3, 5, 7:** Milt & Joan Mann/Cameramann International, Ltd.; **Reader 24, 1:** © Oscar White/Corbis; **2–3:** Library of Congress; **28:** © David Muench/Corbis; **7:** © Bettmann/Corbis; **Reader 25, 1:** Arthur Rothstein/Library of Congress; **3:** © Arthur Rothstein/Corbis; **4:** Dorothea Lange, FSA/Library of Congress; **7:** Library of Congress; **8–9:** Arthur Rothstein, FSA/Library of Congress; **11:** Russell Lee, FSA/Library of Congress; **Reader 26, 1, 5, 7:** © Philip Gould/Corbis; **3:** PhotoDisc; **Reader 27, 1:** Library of Congress; **3:** *The Coming & Going of the Pony Express* by Frederic Remington, The Thomas Gilcrease Institute of American History & Art, Tulsa, Oklahoma; **5:** Culver Pictures Inc.; **7:** © Mary Kate Denny/PhotoEdit; **Reader 29, 1:** NOAA; **3, 5, 7:** NASA

Illustration

Reader 1, 1–7: Morella Fuenmayor; **Reader 2, 1–7:** Mike Dammer; **Reader 4, 1–7:** Jerry Tiritilli; **Reader 7, 1–7:** Gary Krejca; **Reader 8, 3:** Carla Kiwio; **Reader 12, 1–7:** CD Hullinger; **Reader 14, 1–7:** Bobbi Tull; **Reader 15, 1–7:** Bradley Clark; **Reader 16, 1–7:** Donna Catanese; **Reader 17, 1–7:** Toby Williams; **Reader 18, 7:** Carla Kiwior; **Reader 19, 1–7:** Burgandy Beam; **Reader 20, 1–7:** Miguel Angel Luna; **Reader 22, 1:** George Hamblin; **Reader 23, 1–7:** Judy Stead; **Reader 28, 1–7:** Ilene Richard; **Reader 30, 1–7:** George Hamblin

ISBN: 0-328-02302-7

9 10 V0O4 09 08 07 06 05 04

Contents

See Graphic Organizers on pages vi–xii.

Contents

See Graphic Organizers on pages vi–xii.

Unit 5

Take Home Reader 21

Charles Lindbergh, Making History

biography by Ted Jackson
Graphic Organizer Main Idea
Comprehension Skill Drawing Conclusions

Take Home Reader 22

Tokyo Today

expository nonfiction by John Grayson
Graphic Organizer Main Idea
Comprehension Skill Main Idea and Details

Take Home Reader 23

Snowdance

fantasy by Cassie Fricky
Graphic Organizer Event Map
Comprehension Skill Sequence

Take Home Reader 24

Booker T. Washington

biography by Alex Soren
Graphic Organizer Cause and Effect
Comprehension Skill Cause and Effect

Take Home Reader 25

Hard Times on the Farm

narrative nonfiction by Jenna Horton
Graphic Organizer Main Idea
Comprehension Skill Compare and Contrast

Unit 6

Take Home Reader 26

Fiesta Fun

informational article by Antonio Solis
Graphic Organizer Main Idea
Comprehension Skill Main Idea and Details

Take Home Reader 27

The Mail Must Go Through

expository nonfiction by Jared Hull
Graphic Organizer Compare and Contrast
Comprehension Skill Cause and Effect

Take Home Reader 28

Brownies for Breakfast

fiction by Josh Norman
Graphic Organizer Story Sequence 2
Comprehension Skill Drawing Conclusions

Take Home Reader 29

A View from Space

expository nonfiction by Michael Galanzer
Graphic Organizer Main Idea
Comprehension Skill Compare and Contrast

Take Home Reader 30

Outside the Barn

animal fantasy by Nicole Talbert
Graphic Organizer Story Sequence 2
Comprehension Skill Sequence

See Graphic Organizers on pages vi–xii.

Graphic Organizer Story Elements

Title ______________________________

Characters	Setting

Events	Ending

Graphic Organizer Story Sequence 1

Title ______________________________

Characters

Problem

Events

Solution

Graphic Organizer Story Sequence 2

Title ____

This story is about ______________________________

____.

This story takes place ___________________________

____.

The main events are _____________________________

____

____

____.

The story ends when ____________________________

____

____.

Graphic Organizer Main Idea

Title ______________________________

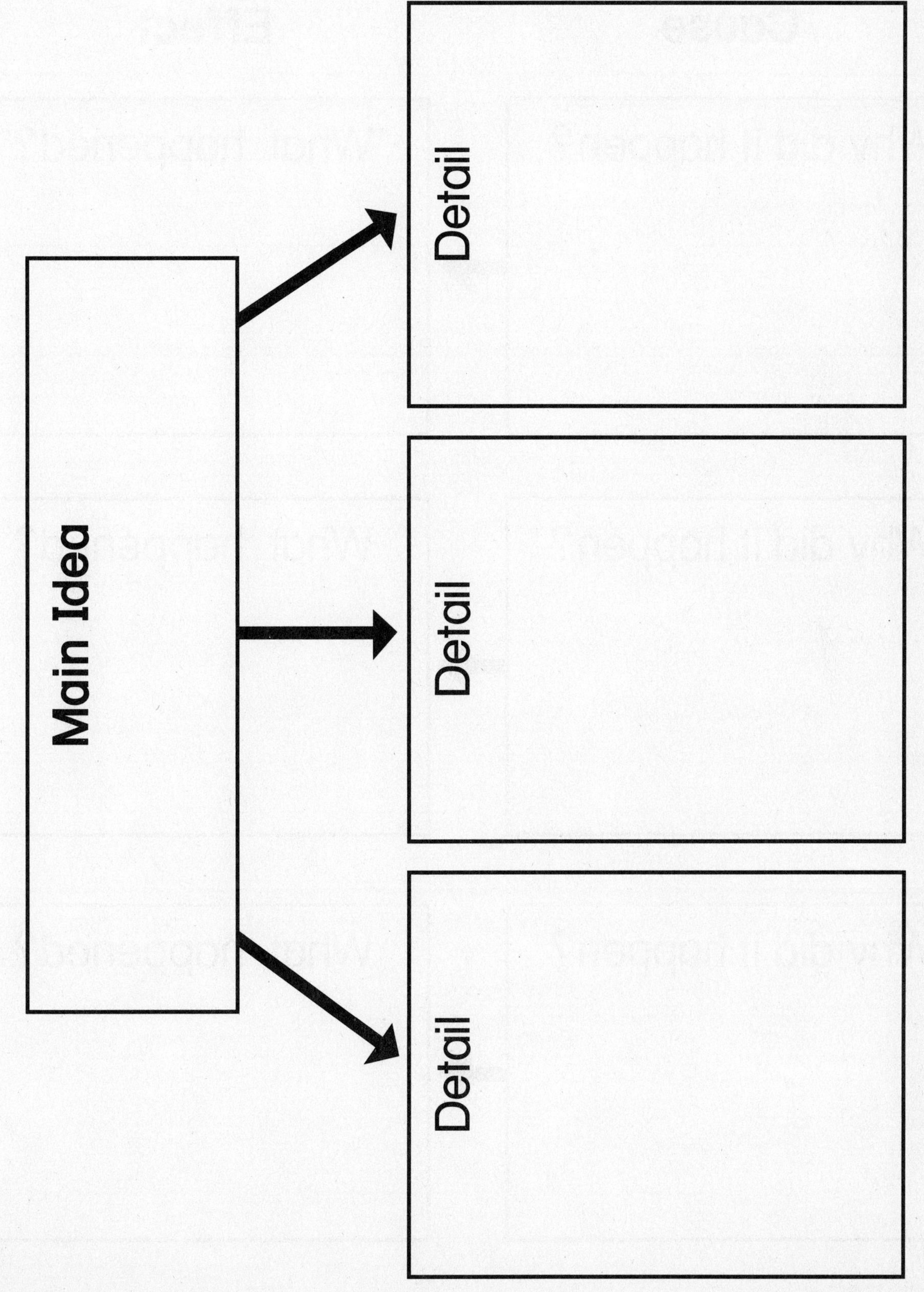

Graphic Organizer Cause and Effect

Title ______________________________

Cause		Effect
Why did it happen?	→	What happened?
Why did it happen?	→	What happened?
Why did it happen?	→	What happened?

Graphic Organizer Compare and Contrast

Title ______________________________

Topic

What is different?

What is alike?

Conclusion

Graphic Organizer Problem and Solution

Title ______________________________

Problem

↓

Solution

Problem

↓

Solution

I Would Like to Visit a Fantastic Place

Written by Rebecca Weiss

Illustrated by Morella Fuenmayor

What is the best vacation?

Alex came home from school. He put his backpack on the table. He saw a picture on the table. It showed a fantastic place. He had never seen anything like it.

"Mom must be planning our summer vacation!" Alex thought. "I wonder where we will go this year. Maybe we will go to the North Pole."

"I would like to visit the North Pole," thought Alex. "I could see white bears. I could see lots of ice."

"The North Pole will be cold though. Maybe we should go somewhere warm. I would like to visit Hawaii. I could warm myself in the bright sunshine. I could swim with the whales."

"There might be sharks though. I do not want to swim with sharks! I would like to visit a huge city. I could go to a fantastic city."

"The city might have crowds of people though. I would like to…" Just then Mom came in.

THE CITY MOUSE AND THE COUNTRY MOUSE

Retold by Carole Palmer
Illustrated by Mike Dammer

Can a country mouse be happy in the city?

“Welcome to the country, City Mouse. Come have breakfast with me this morning.” City Mouse was hungry. Country Mouse gave City Mouse berries and nuts. He was proud to give this good food to his cousin.

“Is this all you have to eat? I like cheese for breakfast,” said City Mouse.

The cousins stayed in the forest all day. City Mouse didn't have fun. Finally, it was time to go to bed. Country Mouse made City Mouse a bed out of leaves.

"Is this a bed?" asked City Mouse. "At home I have a pillow and a quilt."

Now Country Mouse did not feel proud of his home in the forest.

The next day City Mouse said, "Come with me to the city. I promise you'll have fun!"

After a long trip, they reached City Mouse's house. It was big and warm. City Mouse led his cousin into a room. It was filled with boxes of food.

"Help yourself," said City Mouse.

The mice ate cookies, cereal, and popcorn. Suddenly the door opened. A woman walked in. She began to scream. She chased the mice.

City Mouse raced for a hole near the door. Country Mouse ran as fast as he could to hide with his cousin. They were safe, but Country Mouse shook for a long time.

The Rodeo

Written by Kent Lerrin

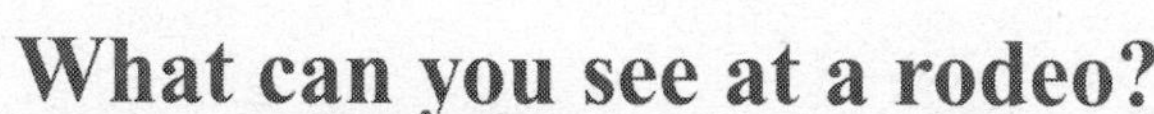

What can you see at a rodeo?

Take Home Reader 3

Cowboys were important in the Old West. They worked on ranches. They were good horse riders. They could tame wild horses. They could catch cattle with a rope. They drove cattle across the land. They took the cattle to market.

You might think there are no cowboys today. But there are cowboys and cowgirls too. Some work on ranches. Many put on great shows. The shows are called rodeos.

The cowboys and cowgirls take part in many events in a rodeo. They try to win prizes.

One rodeo trick is roping. Cowboys and cowgirls use a lariat. *Lariat* comes from a Spanish word. It means "rope."

Cowboys and cowgirls make a loop in a rope. They hold the loop in one hand. They hold the rest of the rope in their other hand. Then they spin the lariat. They spin it over their heads. Some jump through the loop.

Up All Night

Written by Austin Karras
Illustrated by Jerry Tiritilli

What is special about staying up all night?

Characters

Annie, a third-grader
Julia, Annie's best friend

Setting: Annie's house

Time: Night

Scene 1

ANNIE: I'm glad your mom let you sleep over!

JULIA: Me too! What do you want to do?

ANNIE: Let's do something special together.

JULIA: I've got a great idea! Let's stay up all night!

ANNIE: Yes! It will be our secret.

Scene 2

JULIA: *(smiles)* This is a good secret. We can play games all night.

ANNIE: I have lots of board games. But maybe we can watch a video. I have some great movies.

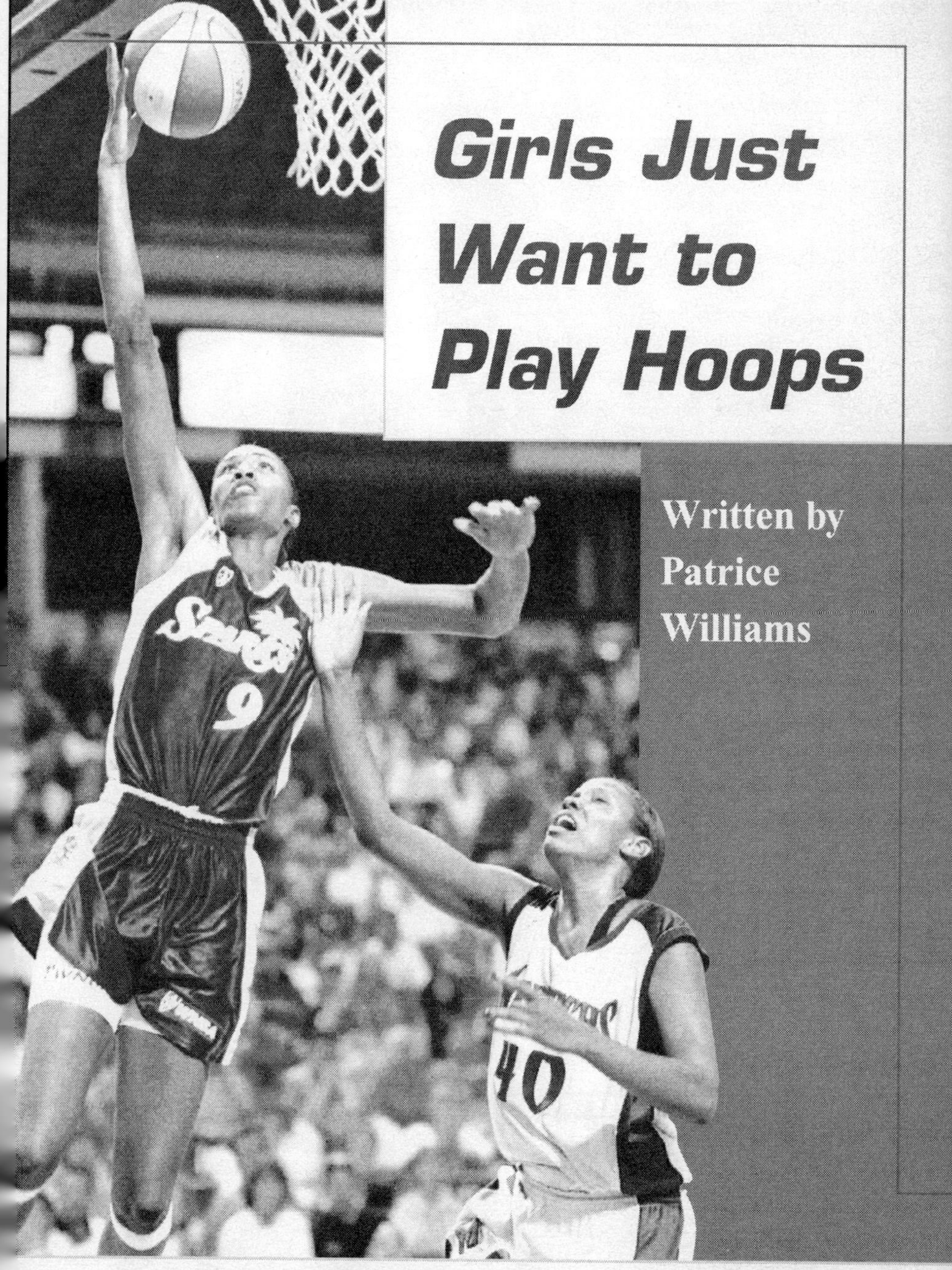

Girls Just Want to Play Hoops

Written by Patrice Williams

Why are women basketball players so happy?

Comets

Do you play basketball? Sheryl Swoopes does. She has played the game for a long time. She played with her brothers. She learned to shoot the ball. She threw the ball toward the basket again and again. She practiced hard. Soon she became a good player.

Sheryl played basketball on her high school team. She played in college. She played on the U.S. Olympic team.

She became a professional player. People pay her to play the sport. She made it to the top.

◀ **Sheryl plays professional basketball for the Houston Comets.**

22
WNBA

Sheryl is a good player. She knows how to shoot. She can move the ball on the basketball court. She knows the game. She has many fans. One company even named shoes after her. They were the "Air Swoopes."

Professional sports teams find the best players. They pay them to play. Men have played professional basketball for a long time. Many cities have professional men's teams.

◀ Sheryl plays hard during the game.

Sheryl dreamed of becoming a professional. But there were no professional teams for women in the United States. Women could play professional basketball in other countries. Sheryl played for a team in Italy. But she wanted to come home. She wanted to play basketball in the United States.

Many people asked why there were no professional teams for women. Girls played in grade school. They played in high school. Women played in college. They played in the Olympics. In 1996 the American women's team won the gold medal!

PLANT TRAPS!

Why do some plants trap bugs?

Written by Corinne Jones

Have you cared for a plant? Do you have plants in your house? Do you have flowers in your yard? You know what a plant needs. It needs light and water. It needs good soil. But some plants need a strange food. Insects are their food!

Plants need minerals to grow. Minerals come from the soil. But some plants live in poor soil. So they get the minerals somewhere else. They get them from insects.

Pitcher Plant ➤

One interesting plant is a Venus flytrap. Can you guess what it eats? It eats flies and other insects. Its leaves have sharp points. Each leaf can open and close.

A fly lands on a leaf. The leaf closes, and the fly is stuck. The fly tries to get away. But the leaf just closes tighter. Then the Venus flytrap digests the fly. It uses the minerals from the fly's body.

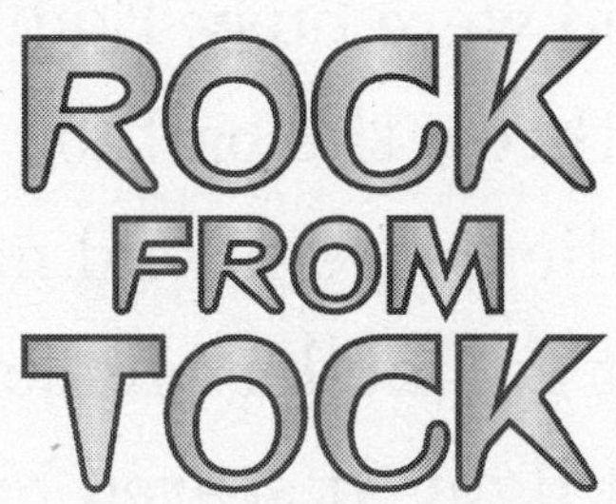

Written by Teresa Jardin
Illustrated by Gary Krejca

Can someone from another planet help a bored boy?

Eddie was bored. His friends in the neighborhood were busy. Eddie wanted someone to throw the ball to.

Then Eddie heard a loud noise. *Hmmmm!* It got louder and louder. Eddie saw a bright light. It scared him. He covered his ears and closed his eyes.

Eddie slowly opened his eyes. He saw someone. But it was not someone from Eddie's neighborhood. This person was green all over. He had bright eyes like flashlights.

"Who are you?" asked Eddie. He was not scared. Now he had someone to play with.

"I'm ROCK and I'm from the planet TOCK. I will be your helper. How can I help you?"

"You could throw the ball to me," said Eddie.

"Great!" said ROCK.

Eddie and ROCK played for a long time. Eddie was not bored now.

“How can I help now?” asked ROCK. His eyes shone like flashlights.

“I have to clean my room,” said Eddie.

“Great!” said ROCK. Eddie led him to his room. Soon Eddie’s room was very neat. It had never been so clean.

“What now?” asked ROCK.

“I have to use the computer to do my homework,” said Eddie.

What is dangerous about a tornado?

Watch Out for Twisters!

Written by Nicholas Riis

You have most likely seen many storms. The sky turns dark. The wind blows. Rain pours down. This is a rainstorm. But there are many kinds of storms. Some are very dangerous. One of the worst storms is a tornado. It is also called a twister.

Weather forecasters warn people about storms. They know how storms build. They look for signs of storms. Storms form high in clouds. A layer of cool air meets warm, wet air. The warm air moves up. It begins to spin. This could lead to a tornado!

How does air move in a twister?

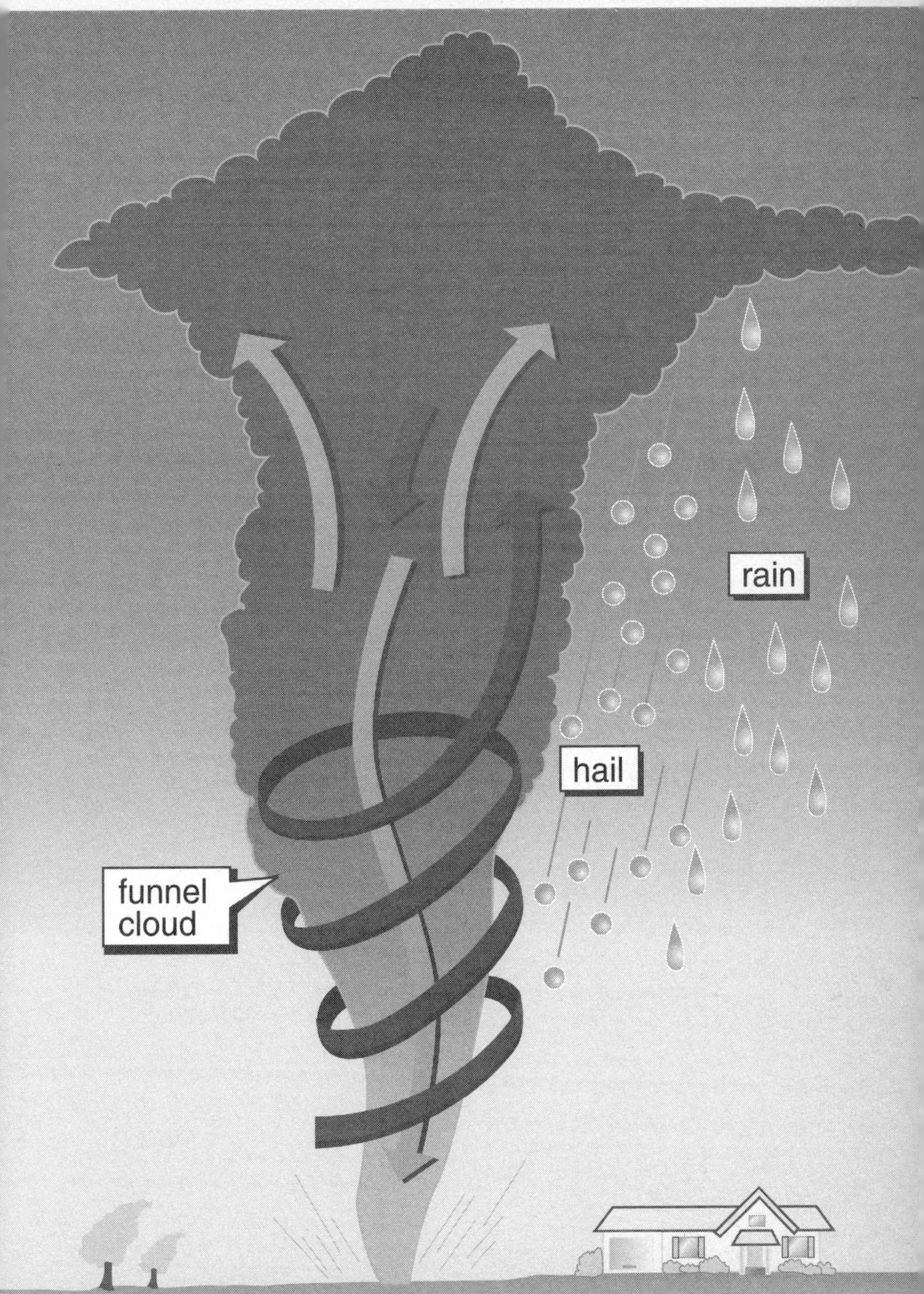

rain

hail

funnel
cloud

A tornado starts as a big black cloud. The air in the cloud spins. Rain may come from it. The wind roars. The cloud forms a funnel. It spins fast. Soon it comes down to the ground. There it picks up dust and trash.

Most tornadoes are in spring. Some places have many of them. Kansas and Oklahoma may have as many as 200 a year. But a tornado can start anywhere.

Tip of the Iceberg

Written by Matt Stratton

The tip of an iceberg! What is it?

It's only "the tip of the iceberg"! Have you ever heard people say this? What did they mean? Let's look at icebergs to find out.

Icebergs are pieces of ice in the ocean, or sea. They may be very large. They may be the size of a city. They can also be very tall. Some icebergs are as tall as skyscrapers.

This iceberg is shaped like a triangle. ▶

Where do icebergs come from? They were once part of a **glacier.** Glaciers are thick areas of ice on land. They cover land in very cold places. They go on for miles and miles. The glaciers do not melt very much. The ice does not become water.

Glaciers move slowly across the land. They slide toward the ocean. When they reach the sea, big pieces break off. They crash loudly into the ocean. These pieces are icebergs.

Icebergs float. They stay near the top of the water. But only a small part of an iceberg shows above water. This part is the **tip** of the iceberg. The rest of it is under the water. That part may be much bigger than the tip. It may also reach deep into the ocean.

Can the water be a home for birds?

BIRDS OF THE WATER

Written by Chandler Grant

Some birds are water birds. They live on or near water. Penguins are water birds. Puffins, sea gulls, and flamingos are water birds too. What are these birds like? How do they raise their young?

Penguins

Let's start with penguins. They spend most of their time swimming in the sea. Penguins are great swimmers. They cannot fly. They use their wings to swim.

How do penguins raise their chicks? Penguins raise their chicks on land. First, the mother lays eggs. Then the eggs hatch. *Hatch* means "break open." The chicks are inside.

The parents care for the chicks. They feed the chicks fish. The chicks grow bigger. Then the parents and chicks swim out to sea.

A penguin chick stays close to its parents.

Puffins

Now let's look at puffins. Puffins are black and white, like penguins. They are also good swimmers, just like penguins.

Puffins catch fish to eat. They use their bright bills. They can catch many fish at once.

Puffins live on the sea. They come to land only once a year. They come to land to raise their chicks.

Where do puffins raise their chicks? First they dig holes in the ground. These holes are called burrows. The puffins build nests inside them.

This puffin has caught a small fish.

Puffins lay their eggs in these nests. Then the eggs hatch and the chicks come out. The parents bring fish to the chicks in the burrow. Sometimes the chicks come out. Then they are in danger. Bigger birds might catch them. The chicks should stay in their burrow.

The puffin chicks, or pufflings, grow. After a while they are ready to fly. These young puffins wait for night. Then they take off for the sea!

Out at sea, the young puffins are on their own. They must learn to swim. They must learn to catch fish. They have started a great adventure!

Making Pictures for a Book

Written by Mark Stanczak

How do pictures get into storybooks?

Do you draw lots of pictures? What do you think about first? What will you draw? Will you use paints or crayons? Some artists make pictures for picture books. They are called illustrators. Illustrators think about these things also.

Sometimes illustrators write the story and draw the pictures. Sometimes they only draw the pictures for a story.

First the illustrator must think. What do the people in the story look like? What do they wear? Where does the story take place? What do things look like?

This illustrator uses paints and pencils. ➤

Illustrators must plan each picture. Will a person be close up? Or will this person be far away? Will everything fit on the page?

Illustrators must choose colors for their pictures. Will bright colors look better for the story? Will dark colors look better? Will they use paints, pencils, or crayons?

Then an illustrator makes drawings. The illustrator shows them to the writer. The writer looks carefully at them. Then the writer may ask the illustrator to change the drawings. The writer may say, "Make the colors brighter. Make the puppy smaller."

This writer works on a new story for children. ➤

The Rabbit and The Turtle

Can a turtle race a rabbit and win?

Retold by Matt Stratton
Illustrated by CD Hullinger

It was spring. The grass was green. It was warm and sunny. A rabbit sat near the road. He wanted to have some fun. Then he saw a turtle.

"This will be fun," he said. He walked toward the turtle.

"Nice day, isn't it?" he said.

"It's a beautiful day," said the turtle. "The sun feels great on my shell."

"It's a great day for a race," said the rabbit. "How about it? Let's run to those pine trees."

The turtle knew he was not fast. He had short legs. The rabbit had long legs. But the turtle was steady. He could work hard.

"I will race you," said the turtle.

Soon many animals came around. They knew the rabbit. They had heard his boasts.

"Do you see the curve in the road?" asked the rabbit. "We will run around it. We will run to the pine trees."

The wise old fox said, "Go!"

Some Special Dogs

Written by Katia Orinski

How do guide dogs help people?

THEATRE ELECTRONICS
duane

A dog can be a great friend. A pet dog can run with you. It can play catch. Some dogs can do even more. They can be helpers. Some dogs help care for sheep. Some find lost people. Some pull sleds. Other dogs help in a different way. They help people who cannot see. They help the people go places. They are **guide dogs.**

Not all dogs make good guide dogs. German shepherds and golden retrievers make good guide dogs. They learn fast. They are calm. They want to make their **owners** happy.

◀ A German shepherd helps its owner cross the street.

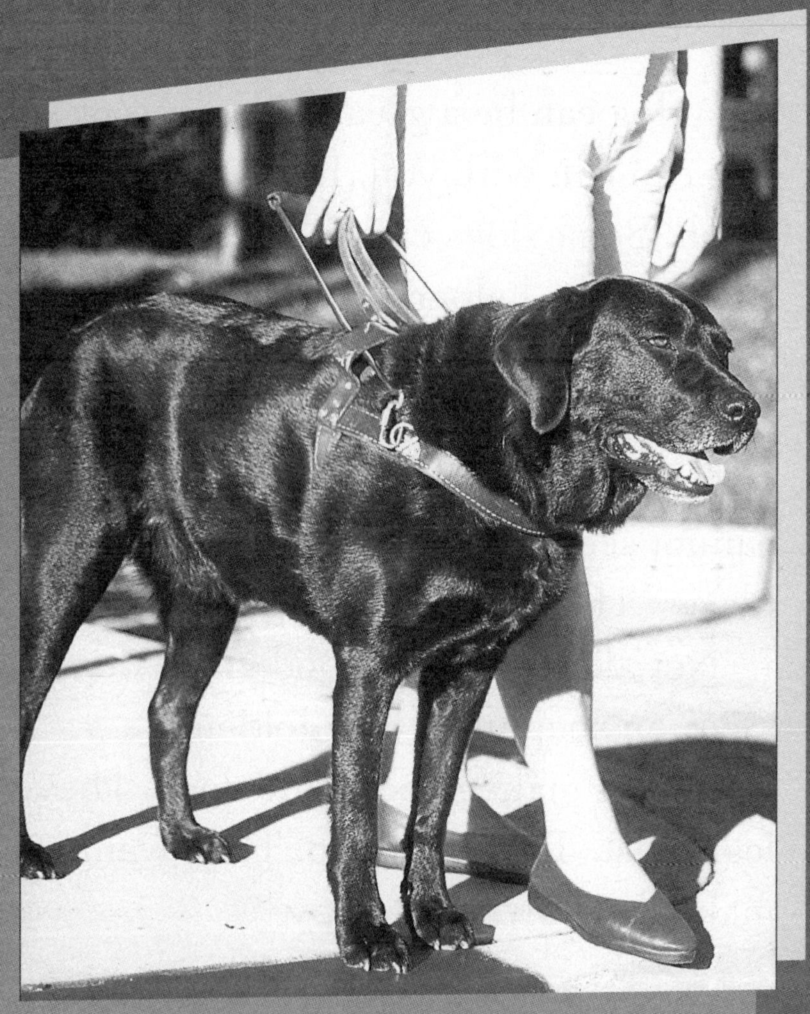

PRETEND YOU'RE NOT AFRAID

Written by
Sarah Whitney

Illustrated by
Bobbi Tull

Lions! Elephants!
Giving a speech!
Which scares you most?

Kate sat at the table. It was a sunny morning. But Kate did not look very happy.

"What are you thinking about?" asked Mom.

"I am thinking about lions and elephants. I am afraid," said Kate.

"That's silly," said her big brother Matt. "Why are you afraid of those animals?"

"I am not afraid of the animals. I am doing a report on the animals. I am afraid of the report," said Kate.

"You're very good at reports," said Mom.

“This is different,” said Kate. “I have to stand in front of everyone. I have to give a speech. It is about animals in Africa. I’m afraid. I might forget what to say.”

"Sometimes I give a speech at my company," said Mom. "I used to be afraid. Then I learned something. I look at each person in the big room. I know many of the people. They are my friends. Then I feel better."

GOOD GAME!

Why is it important to try hard?

Written by Alex Soren
Illustrated by Bradley Clark

It was a cool fall day. Rain was falling. Meg ran out on the soccer field. Meg liked soccer. She loved running and kicking the ball. She did not like being cold, though. She did not like getting wet.

Meg saw Mom, Dad, and Gran. They came to every game. They liked to see Meg try hard. They always cheered for her team.

Meg stood on the wet field. It was cold. Meg wished she didn't have to play. She did not want to try hard today. Soon someone scored a goal. Everyone cheered. Meg stood and just shivered.

Soon it was half-time. "Good game!" said the coach. She said Meg could sit down. But it was even colder on the bench. She sat and shivered more than ever.

Finally, the game was over. Meg's team did not win. The girls were sad and wet.

Meg jumped off the bench. She ran to meet Mom, Dad, and Gran. She wanted to get warm. She was hungry. She wanted a nice snack.

Gran hugged Meg. "Your team played well," she said.

"Give me five!" said Dad.

But Mom did not look happy. "Did you like the game, Mom?" Meg asked.

"Yes. But I thought you would try harder. The team needed your help."

"I don't think I like soccer anymore," said Meg.

Can you make soup with a stone?

Retold by Graham Heckert

Illustrated by Donna Catanese

A long time ago, two brothers left home. Alan and James wanted to find work. Their family was very poor.

They said good-bye to their family. They walked and walked. Suddenly, one brother saw a stone. He picked it up and held it to the brilliant sunlight. The stone sparkled. "One day we will put this stone to good use," he said to his brother.

Many hours went by. The brothers were hungry. Their stomachs were empty. At last, they came to a town. They asked everyone for work or food. They were told, "No work! No food to share!"

They decided they had to find a way to get food. Alan had an idea. He said, "We will make soup."

James said, "But we have nothing to put in soup."

"We'll make stone soup!" Alan exclaimed. James just shook his head. But he helped Alan build a fire.

Soon a woman asked what the brothers were doing. Alan said, "We want to make soup. But we need a pot."

The woman said, "I have a pot. You can use it. But you will have to give me some soup." The brothers agreed.

Soon, everyone in town gathered around the fire. The brothers smiled. "We are making stone soup! We will have a great feast. Please join us as our guests."

Dragons for Breakfast

Will Scott find the golden dragon?

Written by
Rob Zaconi

Illustrated by
Toby Williams

Every morning Scott eats dragons. He eats Red Dragon Delight cereal. Today he read the box. It said, "Find the Golden Dragon. Be the Lucky Winner!" The prize was $100.

Scott could understand how much money that was. Every day he walked a neighbor's dog. For this job he earned $5.00 each week. "$100! That's five months of dog walking," thought Scott.

"Can we buy another box?" he asked his father.

"Sure," said Dad. "I need a few things at the grocery store. Let's go."

Scott found the Red Dragon Delight cereal. There were so many boxes. He took one down. He shook it. He listened to the cereal rustling. Could this box have the golden dragon in it? Scott shook another box. He heard the same sound.

100%
Whole Wheat
100%
Whole Wheat
New
Red Dragon Delight
Find the Golden Dragon
Be the Lucky Winner!
New
Red Dragon Delight
Find the Golden Dragon
Be the Lucky Winner!
Corn Flakes

"Don't shake the boxes!" scolded the store manager. Scott was startled by his loud voice. He put the box back on the shelf.

"I'm looking for one special box," Scott said. "It has a golden dragon in it. If I find it, I win $100. I promise to shake each box gently. I will put each box back on the shelf."

The manager smiled. "I must have startled you. You can shake a few boxes, but not all!"

Scott appreciated the manager's help and thanked him. He chose a few boxes to shake. They all sounded the same. He gave up his search.

"Wait!" called the manager. "Here's another box."

THUNDERSTORMS

Written by Antonio Solis

Thunderstorms: What are they?

The sky is dark. Rain begins to fall. You see a bolt of light flash across the sky. You hear a low rumble. Then you hear a loud crash. You jump. This is a thunderstorm.

A thunderstorm is exciting weather. It brings thunder and lightning. Dark clouds spread across the sky. Heavy rains fall.

It takes time for a thunderstorm to form. It also takes certain weather conditions.

Thunderstorms often happen on warm days. The day may start out sunny. The sun heats the air. The warm air rises. New clouds form. These clouds grow bigger and taller. There is cold air above the clouds.

In time, the warm air bumps against the cold air. This causes the clouds to change. Raindrops and bits of ice form in them. The clouds grow bigger and bigger. They get darker. Soon strong winds begin to blow. Rain begins to fall. It starts to rain very hard. Lightning streaks across the sky. It's followed by the loud booms of thunder.

Lightning causes thunder. Lightning is electricity in the sky. It is very hot. When it flashes, things happen fast. The air around the lightning bolt gets very hot. As a result, the air moves quickly. It spreads out very, very fast. This causes loud explosive noises. The noises are the sounds of thunder.

The Raja's Contest

Retold by Andrea Green
Illustrated by Burgandy Beam

Can someone shorten a line of rice without touching it?

Long ago a raja ruled a land in India. A raja is a kind of king. This raja's land was called Punjab. The raja was kind and wise. Every year he held a thinking contest on his birthday. This was his decree. Every year the order was carried out. This year the raja wanted a special contest. He thought and thought.

He had large pillows. He had thick blankets. But he could not sleep. He did not eat his meal of meat and fish. He called for his helper and ordered, "Just some tea and rice, please."

The helper returned with a pot of tea. He also brought two bowls of rice, a double helping. The raja looked at the two bowls. Then he thought. "I've got it!" he exclaimed.

The next morning, everyone went to the palace. The raja spoke. "I have made a single line of rice. It is fifty grains long. There is one grain for each year of my life." Then he said, "The person who makes this line shorter will win a great reward."

Everyone laughed. That would be easy. A boy named Akbar agreed. "This contest is not special," he thought.

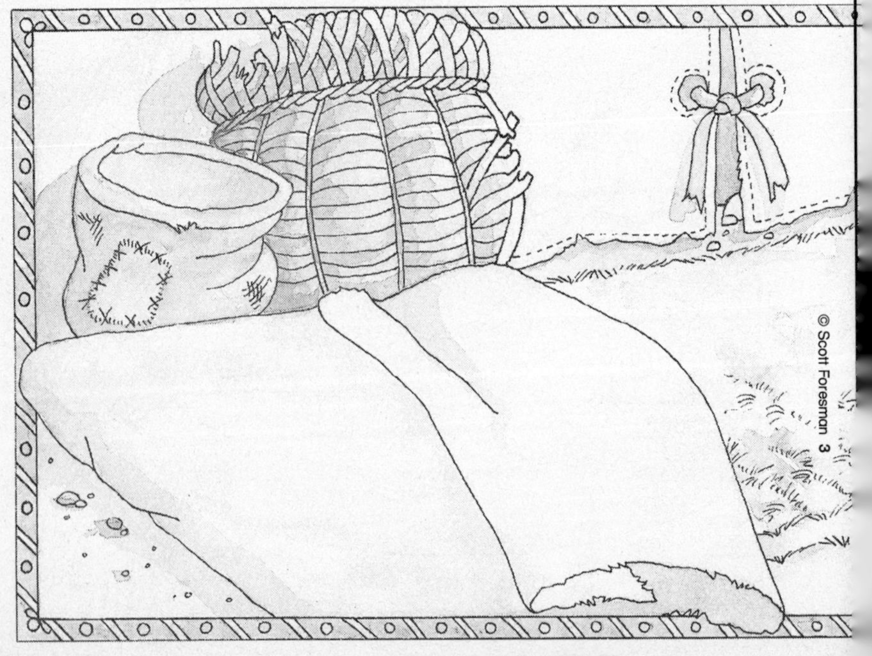

THE TALE OF RETAW YOB

Written by Mario Espinosa
Illustrated by Miguel Angel Luna

Can Retaw Yob put out the fire?

It was a hot, dusty day. A stranger rode into town. He sat tall on his large white horse. Retaw Yob had arrived in town.

Everyone in town stopped to look at him. He looked friendly. He had a big smile. "Howdy," he said. He spoke to everyone. Everyone greeted the man with the strange name.

Retaw got off his horse. He gave it some water. He spoke to some children. He patted a dog on the head.

"I heard you could use some help," he said. "I heard about the fire no one can put out. Don't worry. Your troubles are over. I can put out the fire on Fire Mountain."

Everyone was astonished. It did not seem possible. Even Big Mike couldn't put out the fire. He could not carry enough water. The fire had been burning for a long time. Smoke was everywhere.

Retaw said again, "I can put out the fire. I can do it faster than anyone else."

Big Mike stepped forward. "I respect what you say. I have tried to put it out, but it just keeps burning. I will keep trying. I am Big Mike! I can put it out faster than anyone else."

"Maybe you can," said Retaw, "but I know I can. I can even do it backwards."

Excitement ran through the crowd. They shouted, "You can race!"

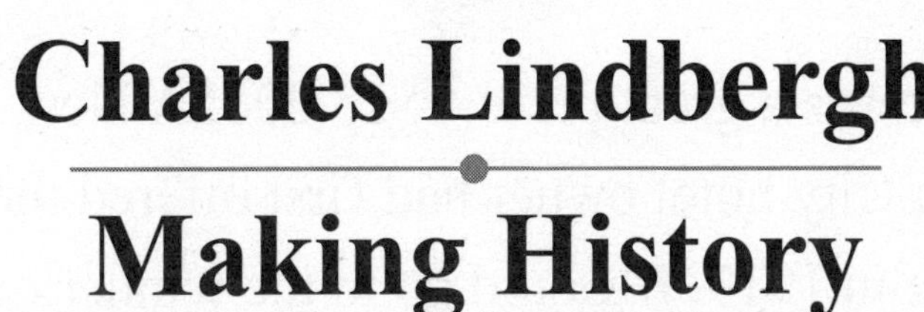

Charles Lindbergh Making History

Written by Ted Jackson

Could Charles Lindbergh fly alone across the Atlantic?

It was a great prize—$25,000! A New York City hotel owner had first offered the prize in 1919. It would go to the winner of a flying contest. To win, a pilot had to fly between New York and Paris. The flier had to make the trip without stopping. Six people tried. No one could complete the route, the trip between New York and Paris. Charles Lindbergh believed he could do it. He wanted to fly across the ocean.

Charles Lindbergh had been flying airplanes for a long time. In the United States Army, he learned to be a better flier. His hard work paid off. He was the best pilot in his class.

Charles Lindbergh was 25 years old when he flew alone to France.

Charles Lindbergh worked as an airmail carrier. His mail route was between St. Louis, Missouri, and Chicago, Illinois. It was dangerous work. He had to fly in all types of weather.

Charles Lindbergh stands by *Spirit of St. Louis*, the airplane that he flew to France.

TOKYO TODAY

Japan

Tokyo

Written by
John Grayson

**Do you like crowds?
You'll love Tokyo!**

Japan's Biggest City

Tokyo is the capital city of Japan. It is one of the largest cities in the world. Tokyo is filled with people. They live and work there. It has bright lights and tall buildings. It has stores and theaters. It has parks and schools. There is always something to do. Tokyo is an exciting city.

The streets of Tokyo are always crowded. ▲

The Busy City

Over 8 million people call Tokyo home. It is a very crowded city. It is very busy too. There is a lot of commotion. Cars, buses, and bicycles fill the streets. There is a lot of traffic. The streets are packed. There is a lot of foot traffic too! The sidewalks are always crowded.

Many companies are in Tokyo. Some make cars. Others make TVs or toys. There seem to be too many to count. The streets are lined with tall office buildings. There are banks and restaurants. Many shops and big offices are also here.

Tokyo does not have much room for houses. Many people live in apartments. Most are very small.

The Emperor's Palace

The emperor is an important person in Japan. The emperor has a palace in the city. The palace is only open two days a year. One day is January 2. The other is the emperor's birthday. On these days, people can visit the palace.

In spring, people go to the parks to see the cherry blossoms. ▶

Snowdance

What do snowpeople do when children sleep?

Written by Cassie Fricky

Illustrated by Judy Stead

Finally, the first big snowfall of winter fell. Jamal rushed outside. PLOP! He stumbled into the deep snow.

"Hi, Jamal!" cried Val. She was trudging toward him.

"Want to build a snowman?" asked Jamal.

"Sure. Let's build a snowlady too," answered Val. "We can play now. But later I have an errand to run with my mom. We are going to the library."

"Then let's get started," said Jamal. "Let's make the snowman by this tree."

First, they rolled a huge round snowball. This would be the bottom of the snowman. Next, they made a medium-sized snowball. It was very heavy. It took all of their strength to lift it. They put it on top of the big snowball. Then they rolled a small snowball. This would be the head. They made eyes and a mouth with stones. Finally, they added tree branches for arms.

They also made a snowlady. She was next to the snowman. Jamal found an old cap and scarf in the house. He put the cap on the snowman. Val put the scarf on the snowlady.

Just then, the wind grew stronger. It made howling sounds. Snow whirled in circles. "I'd better leave," said Val. "Mom and I still have that errand to run."

"Good-bye snowpeople. See you tomorrow," they laughed and waved.

That night Val had a dream. In it, the snowman gathered all his strength. He began to move! Slowly, he began trudging toward the snowlady.

Snowman bowed and took off his cap. "May I have this snowdance?"

Booker T. Washington

Written by Alex Soren

People said Booker must not go to school. What did he do?

His Childhood

Booker T. Washington was born a slave. He was never sure of his birth date. It was probably in the spring of 1856. In the early 1800s, slavery was common in the United States. Africans were brought here as slaves.

▲ **A slave might spend long days picking cotton on a plantation.**

They were bought and sold. They were not treated as people. They were treated as property. They had no rights.

Many slaves worked on plantations, or large farms. They worked many hours each day. It was a very hard life.

▲ **This cabin where Booker T. Washington lived stills stands today.**

Booker lived in a small cabin in Virginia. It was very crowded. He had only one shirt to wear. Booker worked hard on the large farm.

The children of the plantation owner went to school. Sometimes Booker carried their heavy books. He saw the children's school.

Hard Times on the Farm

Written by Jenna Horton

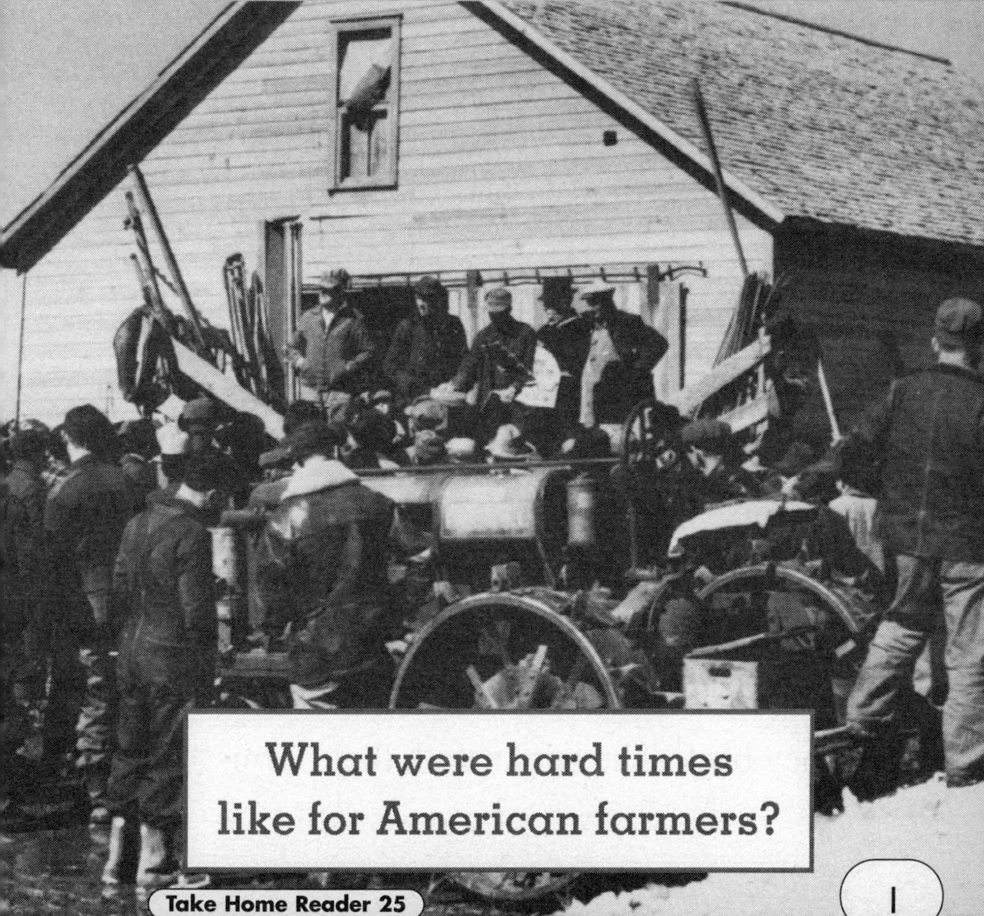

What were hard times like for American farmers?

The early 1900s were good times for American farmers. Farmers could sell their crops and animals for good prices. Some farmers bought more land. Some bought new tractors. They used the tractors to pull plows and wagons. They plowed the land. Their plows turned the soil. Then it was ready for planting. They planted wheat, cotton, corn, and other crops. Some farmers bought more cattle or sheep. They raised their herds. Farmers worked hard to make their farms bigger. Bigger farms meant that farmers could earn more money.

These good times ended in the 1920s. Prices for farm goods went down. Farmers lost money. During the good times, some farmers had borrowed money from banks. The farmers said they would pay the money back. Now they could not pay the borrowed money back. The banks took their farms.

The banks did not need the farms, so they sold them. They held auctions. Auctions are sales in which people bid for things. They say how much they will pay for something. The person who bids the most can buy the item.

People came to auctions to buy farm machines and other things. The price might be low. Look at page 1 to see another auction. ▼

The banks sold everything. They sold tractors, furniture, and dishes. Farmers were forced off their land. They had no money. They did not know how they would live.

Many farm families began to work for others. They went from farm to farm. They asked for work. They were willing to work for very little pay. Even children worked. Children picked crops beside their parents. They worked all day. They did not have time for fun. They did not have time for school.

◀ This young girl helps her family pick cotton.

Everyone hoped things would get better. But they got worse. The Great Depression began. It was a time when business was very slow. Many businesses closed. People lost their jobs. People lost their homes. City streets were filled with homeless people.

Most farmers could not sell their crops. Those who could were offered very low prices. People did not have money to buy anything. Some farmers tried to sell their land and their animals. But most people could not afford to buy them.

Life was very hard for everyone in the country. But it was about to get worse for farmers on the Great Plains.

The sign offers land and a cow for sale. Many farmers tried to sell their land. They needed money for their families. ➤

FIESTA FUN

Written by Antonio Solis

Have you ever played a piñata game?

Our Fiesta Day

I wake to the sounds of excitement. Today is the day of the fiesta, our party. Every year, our city has a party on Cinco de Mayo. It is a holiday in Mexico. But Mexican Americans enjoy this day too. Our whole town comes to the fiesta. We all gather and have fun.

At the fiesta, people dance. They listen to music. They eat outside. But for children, the best part of the fiesta is the piñata game.

A piñata is a decorated pot. This pot is made of clay. It is covered with paper and paste. Piñatas come in many shapes. Many look like animals. The piñata is filled with candies and toys.

We Eat and Dance

During the fiesta, we eat favorite foods. My mother makes a corn dish. We roll cheese in tortillas. We eat sweet bread. We drink hot chocolate.

Fiesta is a time of fun and music. People play music. People dance. They form a large circle. They join hands. They dance to the left. They dance to the right. Everyone has a good time.

In the afternoon, all the children gather. We are very excited. We want to break the piñata and gather up the treats.

The Mail Must Go Through

Written by Jared Hull

Why do people like to get mail?

A pony express rider carried mail in bags on the saddle.

Getting mail is fun. One day you mail a letter. A day or two later, a mail carrier will deliver it. But delivering mail has not always been speedy. It has not always been safe.

In the early1800s, stagecoaches or boats carried the mail. There were no roads. Stagecoaches got stuck in the mud. It took days and even weeks for the mail to be carted, or carried, from one place to another.

In the 1860s, the pony express was started in the West. Young riders rode fast horses. After riding 10 to 15 miles, riders reached a pony express station. Stations were the stopping places for the riders. Here they changed horses in about two minutes. Then they rode off again.

Every rider rode 75 miles or more. Then a new rider took over. They carried mail from Missouri to California. They returned to Missouri with mail. It took 10 days to deliver a letter. The route was about 2,000 miles long.

Pony express helped people get mail fast. People wanted to get mail even faster.

Trains were faster. The first railway post office opened in 1864. Soon railroads stretched from coast to coast.

Workers loaded mail onto mail cars. Clerks sorted the mail. They bundled each town's mail together. Then they put it in a big sack, or mailbag.

Trains did not stop in some towns. These towns did not have stations. But people in these towns could send and receive letters.

Here's how the trains picked up mail.

1. A pole was near the train tracks.
2. A sack of bundled mail hung on the pole.
3. The train raced through town.
4. A clerk on the train grabbed the mailbag with a tool.

Railway workers used a catcher arm to pick up mail. Look at page 1. Find a mailbag on a pole. ➤

Brownies for Breakfast

What's so bad about brownies for breakfast?

Written by Josh Norman
Illustrated by Ilene Richard

The Parker kids were in Ann's room. Ann and Mike were playing checkers. Tim was watching.

"Guess what tomorrow is," said Ann. "It's Mom's birthday. We should do something special."

"Let's take her to a ball game," said Mike.

"Let's take her to the toy store," said Tim. Tim was only five.

"Those are things you like," said Ann. "We need to do something she likes."

Ann patted Tim's head. "I know what," Ann said. "We will make Mom breakfast and bring it to her. She can eat it in bed. I will make eggs. What will you make, Mike?"

“I will make fruit salad,” said Mike. “There is fruit in the refrigerator.”

“Great,” said Ann. “Tim, you can make toast.”

“I don’t want to make toast! Toast is boring,” said Tim.

“But it is easy,” said Ann. “You are too little to make other things.”

“I'm not too little! I want to make brownies!”

“Brownies are not for breakfast!” said Mike. “You can slice bananas.”

“I don't want to slice bananas! I want to make brownies.”

“You can flip pancakes,” said Ann.

“I don't want to flip pancakes,” said Tim. “I want to make brownies. It is Mom's birthday. The brownies can be Mom's birthday cake.”

Ann looked at Mike. Mike looked at Ann.

“Okay,” they said. “You can make brownies.”

A VIEW FROM SPACE

Written by Michael Galanzer

What does Earth look like from space?

Did you ever fly in an airplane? If you looked down, you probably saw little dots. Some dots were houses. Other dots were cars.

In 1961 an American astronaut went into space. His name was Alan Shepard. He had a different view of the Earth. He was too far away to see dots.

In 1968 *Apollo* astronauts said the Earth looked like a big blue marble.

In 1988 and 1990 astronaut R. Mike Mullane took trips on the space shuttle *Atlantis.* A space shuttle is a very important spacecraft. It takes off like a rocket. It has two rocket boosters. They are filled with fuel. The fuel in the boosters helps the shuttle take off. Then they fall off.

For the launch, astronauts wear a special suit. It is heavy. It weighs almost 90 pounds!

▼ **The shuttle takes off.**

The astronauts get on the shuttle about two and a half hours before launch. They lie down. Helpers strap them to their seats. The launch is a rough ride. It feels like a roller coaster.

Soon the shuttle starts to circle Earth. Then the astronauts take off their launch suits. They wear clothes like you wear. But their clothes are a little different. The pockets have to stay closed. That is so things won't float out. Everything floats. Even the astronauts float. They do not weigh much in space. They seem weightless!

Astronauts work outside the shuttle in space. ▶

Outside the Barn

Written by
Nicole Talbert

Illustrated by
George Hamblin

What is wrong with exploring?

Charlie lived in a big barn. He lived with his mother. He had four brothers and sisters. Every morning the sun shone into the barn. Then it was time to explore.

In the barn, Charlie found the biggest stack of hay. He found lots of big tools. He found a very dark corner. It had a huge spider web.

Charlie explored the barn every day. Soon he knew every corner of it. He walked to the barn door and looked outside. What was that tall sparkling thing? Charlie walked outside the barn. There was so much to explore!

Suddenly Charlie felt gentle teeth on his neck. It was his mother.

"I want to see what's outside," said Charlie.

"You are not big enough," said his mother. "There are dangerous things outside the barn."

"But I have seen everything here. I will just look nearby. I will stay close."

"You can go outside, Charlie. But you must stay in our neighborhood. You cannot go into the children's playground. You cannot go into Mrs. Clark's garden. And, of course, you cannot go into Skip's doghouse."

A garden? A playground? A doghouse? Charlie could not believe it. The world had lots of things! Charlie promised to stay in the neighborhood.

He played there all morning. He was happy. Then he saw something sparkling in the sun. He would see what it was. He would be right back.

The sparkling thing was very long. Part of it was up high. Charlie walked behind it. There were steps! Charlie could climb steps. Charlie climbed to the top. He would sit there for a while. Whoops! The sparkling thing was very slippery. Charlie landed with a thump in the dirt. He could not catch his breath.

That was enough of the slippery thing. Charlie looked around. He saw bright colors in the grass. They were beautiful. They did not look dangerous. He would just see what they were. Charlie walked toward the tall green stems. On top were bright colors. They were red, yellow, and purple. They smelled good.

Soon Charlie was ready to leave. But there was a problem. He could not find his way out. He walked around for a long time. The good smell was making him dizzy. Finally Charlie saw something sparkling. It was the slippery thing! Charlie knew it was in his neighborhood.

Charlie ran toward it. He did not like being lost. Just then Charlie saw a little house. It had a little round door. Maybe he would just see what was inside. He peeked into the house. It was dark. He walked inside.

Oh no!

Skip chased Charlie to the barn. Charlie ran inside just in time. He ran up the steps. Skip could not reach him there. Charlie was very glad to see his mother.

Charlie's mother was angry. "Did you learn anything today, Charlie?"

"Yes, Mom," said Charlie. He had learned a lot. He wondered what he would learn tomorrow.

LOOKING BACK

SKILL PRACTICE

1. Tell about the main parts of the story. Use the story map below.

This story is about ______________________.

This story takes place ____________________.

The main events are _____________________.

The story ends when _____________________.

2. What happened after Charlie got lost?

TALK ABOUT IT

3. Do you think Charlie will stay in the barn from now on? Talk about this with a partner.

As they circle Earth, the astronauts work. They take pictures. They do experiments. Sometimes they even work outside the shuttle. Then they wear a different spacesuit.

Mr. Mullane thinks astronauts don't need TVs. That is because they can watch Earth. Earth looks blue from space. That is because of its many oceans. Astronauts can see clouds from space. The clouds are in many different shapes. Astronauts can also see lightning. They see many flashes each minute. Sometimes the astronauts can see city lights.

The shuttle circles Earth for a few days. Then it is time to return to Earth. The astronauts put their spacesuits on again. The shuttle moves smoothly to Earth.

Would you like to go into space? It is an important job. You would do experiments.

Astronauts can float in the shuttle. ▶

Maybe you can become an astronaut. You must go to college. You must study science and math. You would work hard. Then you can have a special view of Earth. You can see home in a different way.

LOOKING BACK

SKILL PRACTICE

1. This is a nonfiction article. What is the main idea? What are some supporting details? Use the graphic organizer.

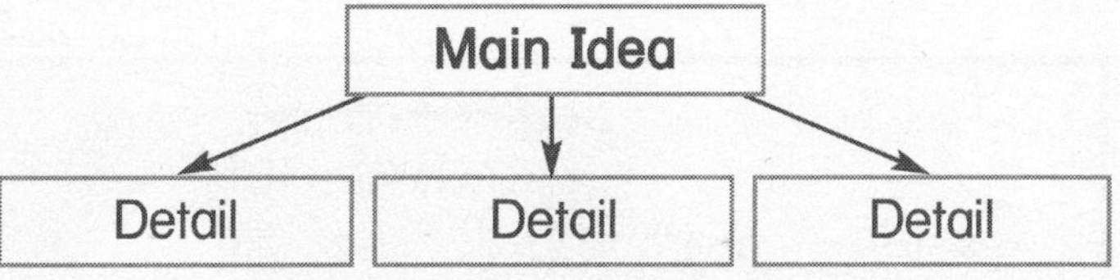

2. Contrast how Earth looks to you and how Earth looks from space.

THINK ABOUT IT

3. Would you like to go into space? Tell why or why not.

It was the morning of Mom's birthday. It was only seven o'clock. But Ann, Mike, and Tim were in the kitchen.

Ann was beating eggs. Mike was slicing fruit. Tim was mixing batter in a bowl. The batter was thick and creamy. It was dark brown.

Mike and Ann helped Tim. Then Ann said to him, “The brownie batter looks good. Maybe your brownies will be a success.”

Soon they stood by Mom’s bed. Ann showed Mom the tray of food.

“What have you kids done?” said Mom. “You made eggs. You made fruit salad. Fruit is good for breakfast. And you made brownies? I have never had brownies for breakfast!”

“I made the brownies!” said Tim. “I went to the kitchen. I opened the package.

I put the mix in a bowl. I got eggs out of the refrigerator. Mike put the eggs in the mix. I stirred and stirred. Then I put the mix in the pan. Ann put the pan in the oven. The brownies cooked for thirty minutes. Then I put a candle in your brownie. It is for your birthday."

Mom loved her breakfast. The eggs were a little burned. The fruit salad was mostly peaches. That was because Mike liked peaches best. But the birthday brownies were perfect. Everyone ate two. The Parkers agreed. Tim's brownies were a big success.

LOOKING BACK

SKILL PRACTICE

1. Tell about the main parts of the story. Use the story map below.

   This story is about ______________________.

   This story takes place ____________________.

   The main events are ______________________.

   The story ends when ______________________.

2. Why did Ann and Mike decide to let Tim make brownies? Tell what you think.

TALK ABOUT IT

3. What would you cook for a special meal? Talk about this with a partner.

The tool was called a catcher arm. The arm was attached to the train.

How did trains leave the mail? Another clerk tossed a mailbag. It landed on the railroad platform. The train never stopped. Mail was delivered "on the fly" to some towns.

What happened to mail for towns that were not near a train station? Workers carted the mail in wagons to these towns. Horses pulled the wagons.

Later motor cars were invented. Then trucks could deliver mail. Delivery time became faster. It cost less to send a letter.

After airplanes were invented, they could carry mail. At first, pilots only flew during the day. Pilots had no radios to help them. They looked for landmarks on the ground. Then they knew where to land.

How do you send mail now? You put a letter into a mailbox. A truck carries it to the post office. A clerk sorts it. The letter travels by truck or airplane to another post office. A mail carrier delivers it to a home, school, or business.

Today, people get mail easily. They get mail quickly. They might get mail every day. Do you?

Trucks carry mail to a post office. ▼

LOOKING BACK

SKILL PRACTICE

1. This article is nonfiction. Compare the different ways that people delivered mail. Use the organizer to help you.

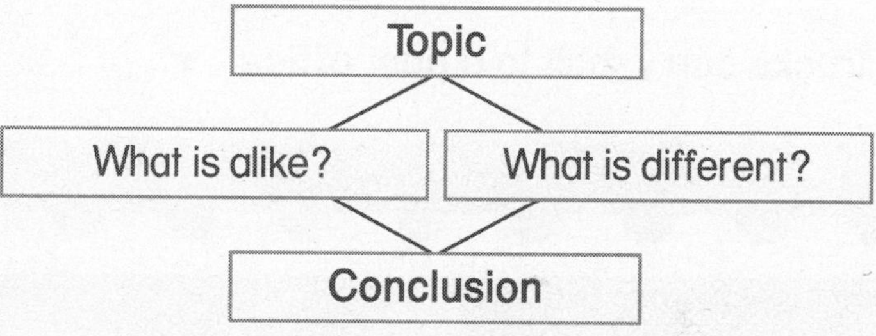

2. Why did people begin to use trains to deliver mail?

THINK ABOUT IT

3. Did using the organizer above help you understand the selection better? Why or why not?

We Play the Piñata Game

We have waited all day for the piñata game. It is called La Piñata. Roberto, my brother, made the piñata.

Roberto put layers of paste and paper around a clay pot. He shaped it to look like an animal. Then he let the piñata dry in the sun. There was a hole in the piñata. He filled the piñata with treats. Then he covered the hole with paper and paste. He covered the whole piñata with crepe paper. Crepe paper is very thin and colorful.

Finally, Roberto calls all the children. He hangs the piñata from a tree branch. He covers Ana's eyes. He gives her a long stick. It has crepe paper streamers on it.

He turns Ana around a few times. He says, "Go!"

Ana swings the stick. She tries to hit the piñata. We count in Spanish. We count in English, "one, two, three." Ana does not break the piñata. Another child takes a turn. At last, a child breaks the piñata. We all try to get the treats.

As night falls, we sit in the yard. We watch fireworks light up the sky. We have enjoyed our fiesta.

LOOKING BACK

SKILL PRACTICE

1. This article is nonfiction. Tell the main idea and some supporting details.

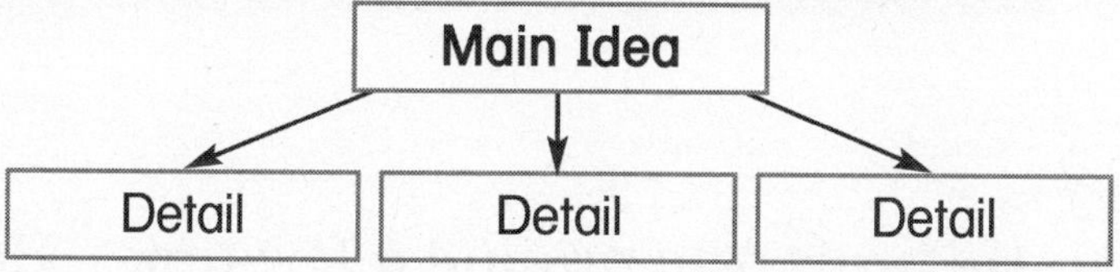

2. The piñata game is fun for children. Give two details that show how it is fun.

THINK ABOUT IT

3. How is a fiesta like a party your family might have? How is it different?

-FOR-SALE-
-THIS-PLACE-AND-COW-

Drought hit the plains in the early 1930s. A drought is a long period of no rain. Everything on the plains became dry. Then windstorms came.

Dust and dirt pile up against farm buildings. ▼

The storms picked up dirt and dust. The air was black with it. Houses were filled with it. It piled up against buildings. The dirt and dust was the rich topsoil from farms. The wind was blowing it away. With it went the farmers' way of making a living. Without rain and good soil, crops would not grow.

These were very hard times. Farmers had no money. They could not raise crops. They had to find work. Some decided they had to move on. Many heard that there was work in California. They packed some of their things in trucks or wagons. Then they took to the roads. Whole farm families headed for California. There they hoped to find good times once again.

In time the government helped farmers. Trees were planted on the Great Plains to hold down the soil. Farmers learned better ways to care for their land. Good times would return.

Many families left their farms. They hoped to find work in another place. ▶

LOOKING BACK

SKILL PRACTICE

1. This is a nonfiction article. Think about the main idea. Name details that support it. Use the main idea map below.

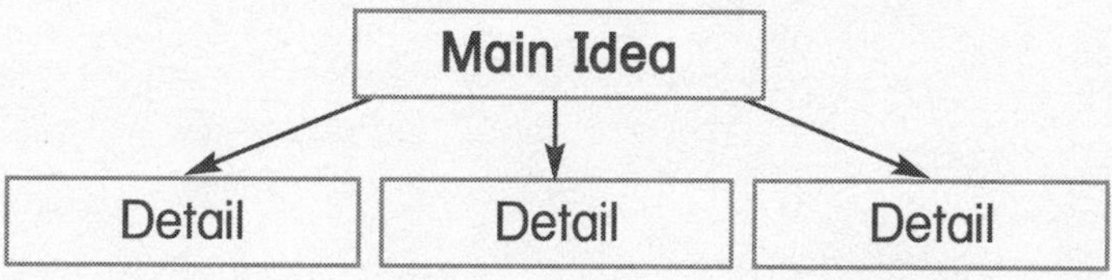

2. How were the early 1900s for American farmers? How were the 1920s and 1930s different for them?

TALK ABOUT IT

3. Imagine that you are a child in a family that lost its farm in the 1920s or 1930s. What would your life be like? Talk about it with a partner.

Booker wanted to learn too. He wanted to learn to read. But slaves were not allowed to go to school.

The Civil War

In the 1860s, Americans fought a war called the Civil War. The Northern states fought against the Southern states. Many people in the South wanted to keep slaves. Others did not like slavery. They wanted it stopped.

In 1865, the Civil War ended. The South lost the war. Slavery was ended. Slaves were now free. Booker's family left the plantation. They moved to West Virginia. Life was still hard. Booker worked all day. But he still wanted to learn. He wanted to learn the alphabet. He wanted to know what words said. He wanted to read newspapers.

School at Last

His mother got him an alphabet book. He did not know the letter sounds. He started to think that he could not learn. Finally, he was allowed to go to school at night. Booker was about 10 years old. He worked hard. At last, he could read!

Six years later, Booker went away to school. He worked while he went to school. Booker believed in learning, working hard, and helping yourself. After he finished school, Booker became a teacher. He wanted to help others get a better life.

His Later Life

In 1881, Booker became the head of a new school. It was called the Tuskegee (tuhs KEE gee) Institute. Here, African Americans learned important skills. Then they could get better jobs.

Booker worked hard. He became an important teacher and leader. He became well-known. Booker T. Washington died on November 14, 1915. Many newspapers carried stories about him and his important work.

Tuskegee Institute offered young African American men a good education. ▼

LOOKING BACK

SKILL PRACTICE

1. This is a nonfiction article about a person. Tell about things that happened to him and why they happened. Use the graphic organizer to help you.

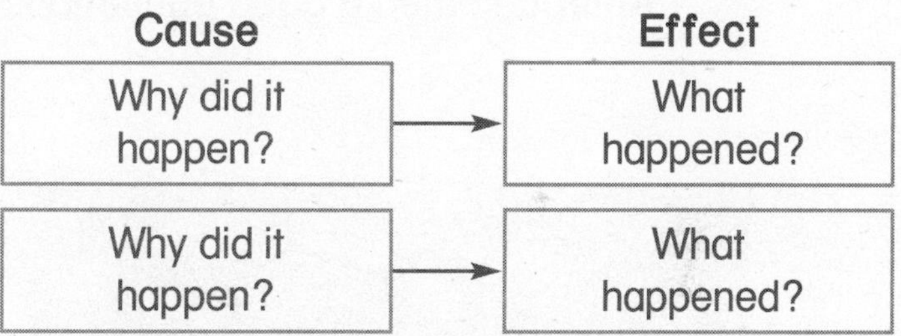

2. Why did Booker not go to school with the plantation owner's children?

THINK ABOUT IT

3. Booker T. Washington thought learning was important. Do you agree? Why?

Snowlady smiled, “I would love to, but there is no music.”

“Of course there is. Don’t you hear it? The howling winds make beautiful music.”

Snowman held out his branches. Snowlady did the same. They whirled and twirled, dancing to the winds. Sometimes slowly. Sometimes quickly. They never stumbled. Snowlady’s scarf blew. The snow fell around them. What a wonderful sight it was!

All too soon, the sun began to rise. The dancers went back to their tree. Then Val woke up. She could not wait to tell Jamal about her dream.

Later, Val and Jamal met outside. They saw their snowpeople. Something was different.

"Wasn't the snowman in front of that tree?" asked Jamal.

"I think so," said Val. "I thought the snowlady was on the other side of him too."

"They're too big and heavy to be moved. We must not be right," they agreed.

"Come on, let's make more snowpeople. Then they'll have friends," said Jamal.

Val laughed. "That's a great idea. Let's get started!"

Snowman and Snowlady thought, "What fun. Tonight there will be more of us. We will have a real snowdance party!"

LOOKING BACK

SKILL PRACTICE

1. In this story, events happen in a certain order. What are the events? Use the organizer to put them in order.

Title ______________________

Event
Event
Event

2. What happens at the end of the story? What events might happen next?

TALK ABOUT IT

3. Could snowpeople really dance? Could Val's dream come true? Talk with a partner.

キリン

The land around the palace is beautiful. There are many gardens and pools of water. Spring is one of the most beautiful times. Flowers and cherry trees bloom. In spring, birds build their nests in the trees. They play and splash in the pools. It is nice here. People can get away from the commotion of the city.

Fun in the City

There is so much to see and do in Tokyo. There are places to eat and shop. People go to plays and movies. They go to museums and libraries. The people like baseball. They also enjoy sumo wrestling, soccer, and golf.

There is even a Tokyo Disneyland! Tokyo is exciting—day or night!

Even at night, Tokyo is a busy city. ▶

クスリ

LOOKING BACK

SKILL PRACTICE

1. This is a nonfiction article. Tell the main idea and supporting details. Use the organizer below to help you.

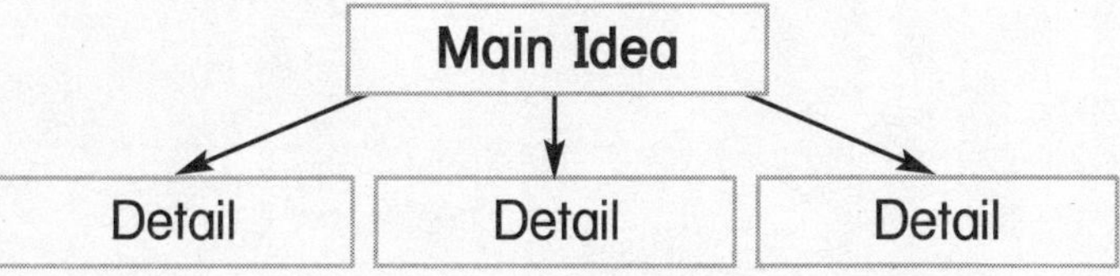

2. The author describes Tokyo as a busy city. What are some details that support this idea?

THINK ABOUT IT

3. Do you look at an article before you begin reading? How can looking at pictures and reading headings help you know what an article is about?

Charles Lindbergh wanted to win the contest. He spent many hours planning. He knew he needed a special airplane. It cost a lot of money to build. Some people in St. Louis wanted to help. They gave him the money he needed. He named his airplane the *Spirit of St. Louis* in their honor.

The airplane had to be just right. It could not be too heavy. Weight would slow it down. A heavy plane used more fuel too. The *Spirit of St. Louis* was built with just one engine. One engine could power the airplane. Another engine would make it too heavy. But Charles Lindbergh made sure the airplane had instruments that would help him find his way to Paris.

The brave pilot also decided to fly alone. Another person added more weight and took up space. He wanted the extra room for a large fuel supply. Finally, the *Spirit of St. Louis* was ready. Charles Lindbergh was ready.

It was May 20, 1927. Charles Lindbergh looked over the airplane. He checked the instruments. They were working just right. Everything was in place.

Charles Lindbergh took off from an airport near New York. He left just before 8:00 in the morning. The flight lasted $33\frac{1}{2}$ hours. It was hard to stay awake so long. But finally, he landed near Paris. He did it! Charles Lindbergh had made history.

The city of New York gave a parade to welcome Charles Lindbergh home. ▶

OFFICIAL
CAR 1

LOOKING BACK

SKILL PRACTICE

1. This is a nonfiction article. Name the main idea. Then add some details that support the main idea. Use the graphic organizer.

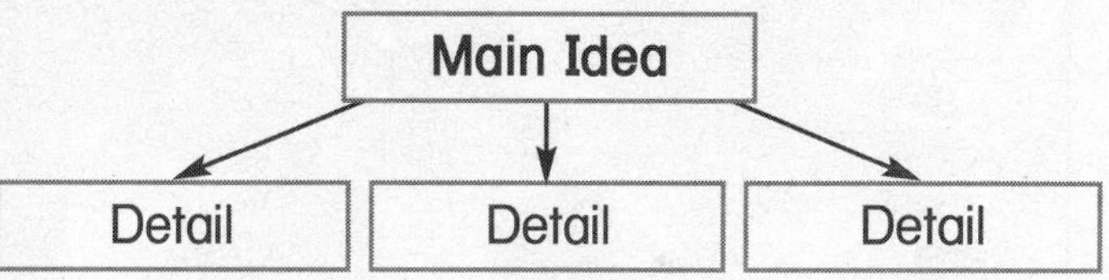

2. Why was the weight of the plane important to Charles Lindbergh?

THINK ABOUT IT

3. Airplanes were a new invention in Charles Lindbergh's time. What new kinds of transportation do you think you will see in your future?

Up the mountain went Big Mike and Retaw. Big Mike walked forward. He carried his washtub. Retaw walked backwards. He carried buckets. They raced up the mountain.

Retaw threw water on the fire and raced down. He was on his third trip. Mike was still on his first. Mike shouted to him, "Retaw, you're making me dizzy. Running up and down the mountain backwards is strange. Can't you turn around? Can't you walk forward?"

"Sorry," answered Retaw. "It may seem strange to you. But backwards is the only way I can carry water."

The hours passed by. People began going home. Before long, everyone in town went to bed. Only Mike and Retaw were awake. They kept taking water up the mountain. They poured lots of water on the fire.

When morning arrived, people came to the mountain again. They wanted to see what had happened during the night. They looked at the top of the mountain. Instead of fire, there was only a little smoke. Retaw and Big Mike had put out the fire!

The townspeople were astonished. "Retaw Yob, you did it!"

"Retaw, you were able to work longer and faster than me," said Big Mike. "You are a hero!"

"Big Mike, I respect you for trying so hard. You're a hero too."

As Big Mike and Retaw shook hands, two strangers rode into town. They told Retaw about a fire in their town. They needed help putting it out. Retaw Yob was just the man to do it!

Hold this page up to a mirror. Do you see clues that tell you what Retaw Yob's name means?

LOOKING BACK

SKILL PRACTICE

1. This story is a tall tale. What happens in the tale? Use the organizer below to help you answer the question.

Characters	Setting
Events	Ending

2. How do you think Retaw learned about the fire on Fire Mountain?

TALK ABOUT IT

3. Both Retaw and Mike raced to put out the fire. Talk with a partner about how the race helped the town.

Then the raja continued, "You cannot touch the rice. You cannot take any grains away."

Now no one thought the contest was easy. Day and night Akbar thought. He could not sleep. He lay awake in his straw bed. Akbar's family had very little food, but they wanted him to have some.

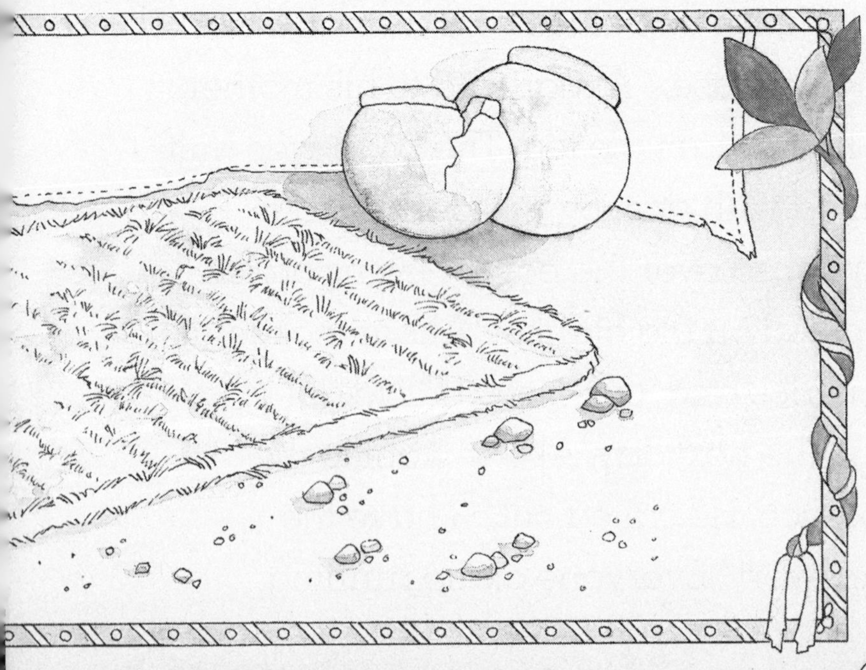

"Just a cup of tea and a small bowl of rice, please," Akbar said to his mother. She brought the tea. The bowl was half-filled with rice. By accident, Akbar knocked over the bowl. Grains of rice spilled on the blanket. Akbar looked at the rice and exclaimed, "I've got it!"

The next day, Akbar went to the palace. He called out, "I have the answer!" Everyone came running.

Akbar knelt down. He made a line of one hundred grains of rice. He put them below the first line. It was double the length. Yes, now the first line was shorter.

The raja was pleased. "Akbar, you've done it. My daughter will reward you."

Akbar was pleased. His reward was great. But he did not care for the money. He fell in love with the raja's daughter. Soon they were married. Everyone in Punjab came to the wedding.

LOOKING BACK

SKILL PRACTICE

1. This story is fiction. Tell what the story is all about. Use the organizer below to help you.

This story is about ____________________.

This story takes place ____________________.

The main events are ____________________.

The story ends when ____________________.

2. How are the raja and Akbar alike? How are they different?

THINK ABOUT IT

3. Do you look at pictures before you begin reading a story? How can they help you understand the story better?

Light and sound do not travel at the same speed. Light travels faster. This means you see lightning first. Later you hear the thunder. The sound of thunder travels one mile in five seconds.

You can tell how far away a thunderstorm is. You must count the number of seconds between lightning and thunder. After you see lightning, begin counting. For example, you count ten seconds. Then you hear thunder. The thunderstorm is two miles away. (Ten divided by five is two.)

Remember to be careful during a storm. Are you outside? Get indoors. Are you indoors? Stay there. That's the safest place to be in a thunderstorm.

Warm air and cool air bump during a storm. ▶

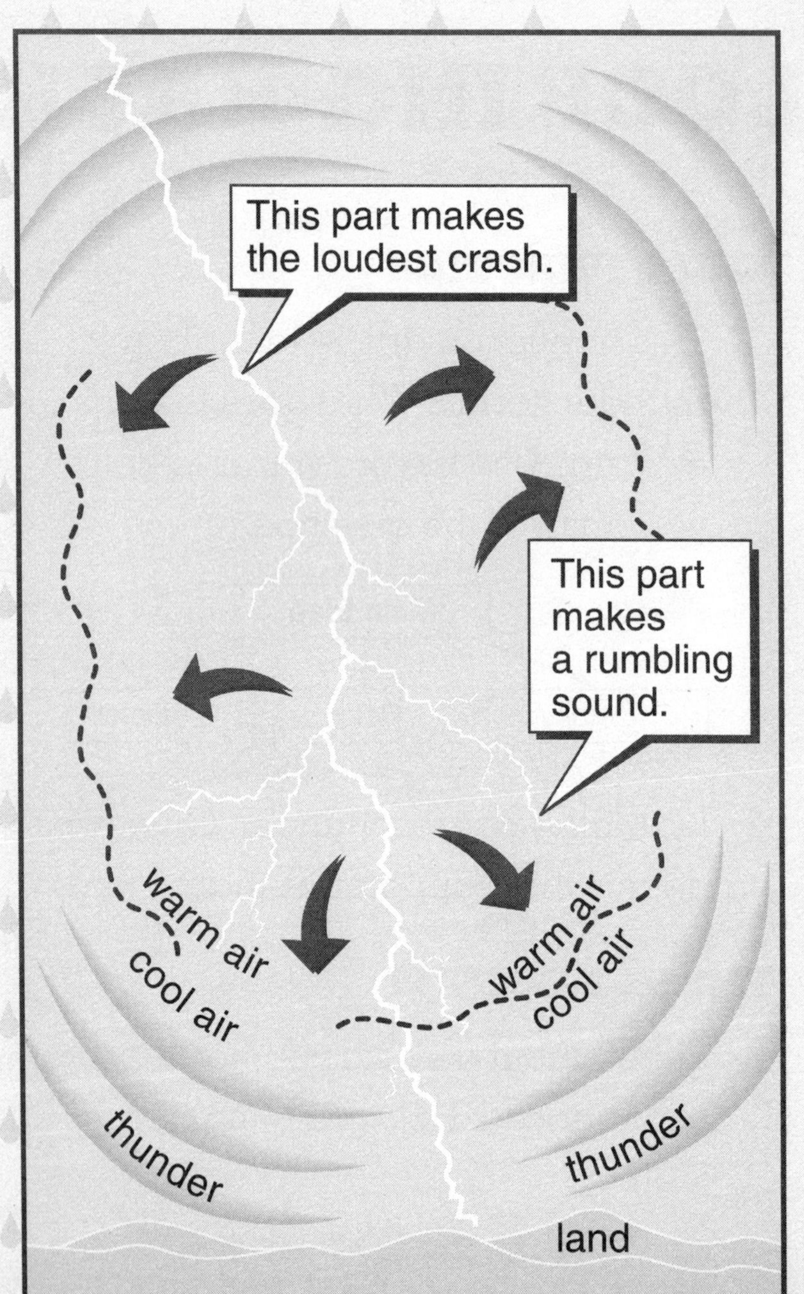
This part makes the loudest crash.
This part makes a rumbling sound.
warm air
cool air
warm air
cool air
thunder
thunder
land

LOOKING BACK

SKILL PRACTICE

1. This nonfiction article tells about thunderstorms. What does the article explain? Use the organizer to help you answer the question.

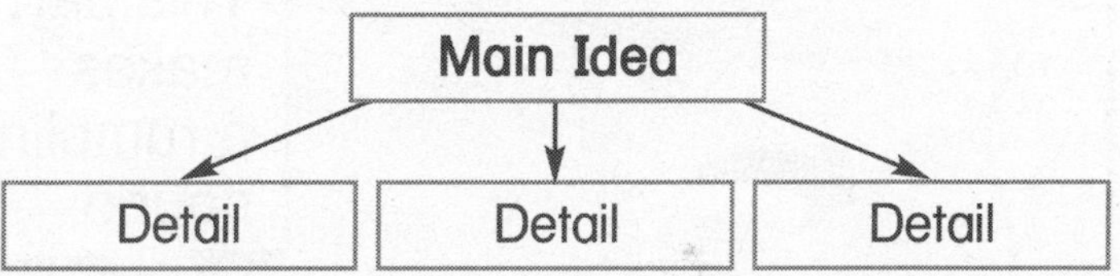

2. Lightning causes thunder. Give two details that support this main idea.

THINK ABOUT IT

3. Think about a storm you have experienced. How did it make you feel?

New
Red Dragon Delight
the Golden Dragon
the Lucky Winner!

New
Red Dragon Delight
Food Pyramid

Scott shook the box. He listened carefully. This one sounded the same. But Scott bought it.

"Thank you so much," said Scott. "I appreciate your help."

"Good luck!" the manager said.

"Okay, this is it! Golden dragon, you're mine!" Scott found all the cereal bowls in the kitchen. He filled each bowl.

Finally, the box was empty. All the dragons were red. But wait. In the bottom of the box was a paper. It read:

Congratulations! You have won a FREE box of Red Dragon Delight.

Scott smiled, "I am lucky. I may find the golden dragon yet. But if I don't, I still have my job walking dogs!"

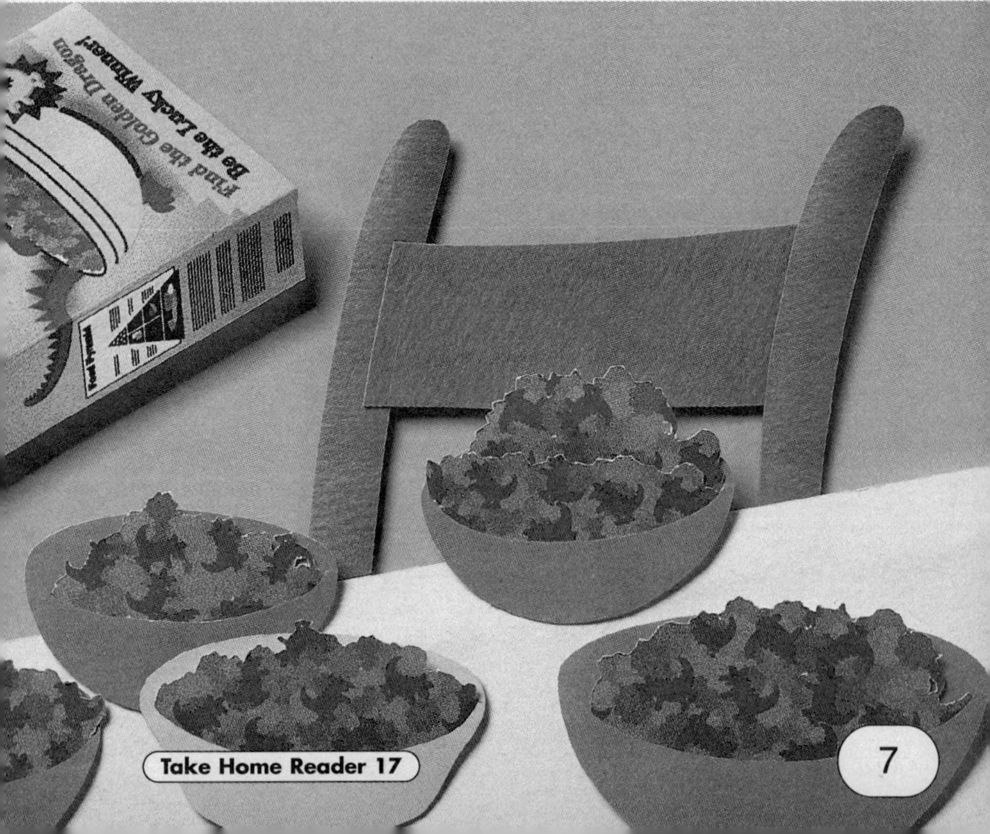

LOOKING BACK

SKILL PRACTICE

1. This story is fiction. What is the story mainly about? Use the organizer below to help you decide.

This story is about ____________________.

This story takes place ____________________.

The main events are ____________________.

The story ends when ____________________.

2. Scott shakes several boxes of cereal at the grocery store. What effect does this have on the store manager?

TALK ABOUT IT

3. Talk with a partner. Do you think Scott will win the cereal contest someday?

"First, we'll need water," said the brothers. Two boys brought water. James poured it into the pot. Soon it was boiling. Then, James dropped the brilliant stone into the boiling water.

"This stone is the secret to our soup," James said.

People in town were very excited to be guests. The soup would cost them nothing. They could enjoy a wonderful feast.

"The soup would have more flavor if we had onions and carrots," said Alan.

"I have onions and carrots," said a woman. "I will share them."

"Meat would add flavor," said Alan.

"And potatoes," said James.

The farmer wanted to share too. "I have some," he said.

Other people brought bread.

"It's ready!" called James and Alan.

Everyone enjoyed the feast. People ate until their stomachs were full. "This was wonderful soup," they agreed. "And all we needed was water and a stone!"

LOOKING BACK

SKILL PRACTICE

1. This story is fiction. What is the story about? Use the story map to help you.

Characters	Setting
Events	Ending

2. What happened after James dropped the stone into the water?

THINK ABOUT IT

3. People in the story share their food to help make the soup. Tell about a time you shared something. How did it make you feel?

Meg did not talk in the car. At home she went to her room. She did not even have a snack.

Soon someone came into the room. It was Gran.

"You don't seem happy," said Gran.

"I'm not happy," said Meg. "Mom is not happy with me. She wants me to play better. Gran, I don't like playing in the rain. But I do like to play soccer."

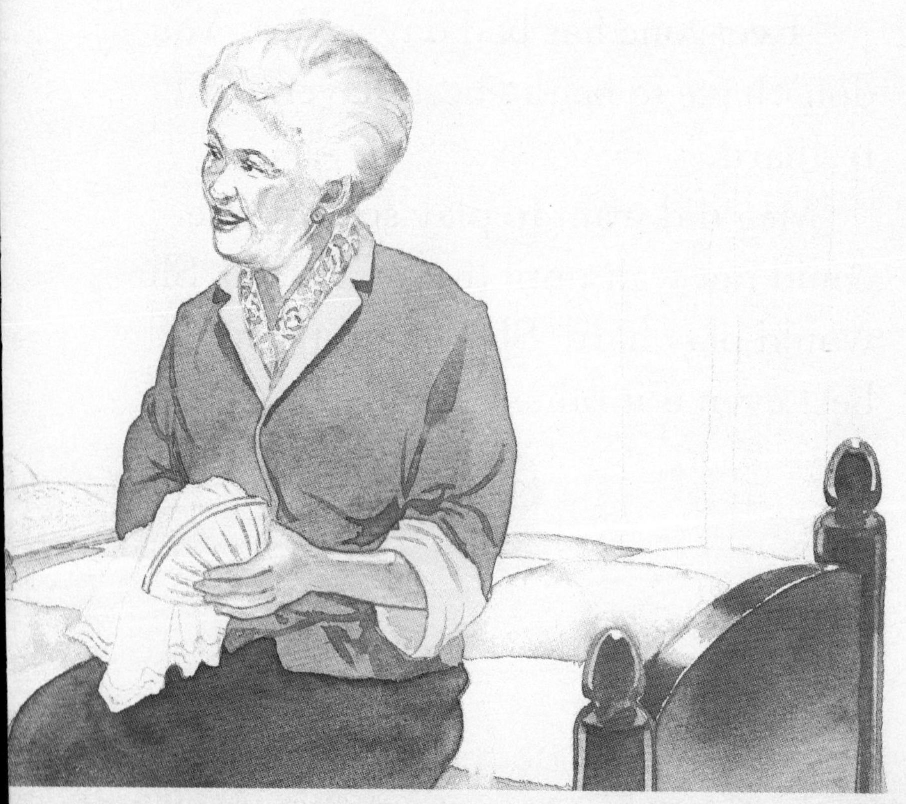

"Long ago your mom liked soccer. She was a good player. She played hard," said Gran. "You are a good player. Your mom wants you to help your team."

Meg went to her mom and hugged her. "I should have run more. Then I would have stayed warm," Meg said.

"Everyone has bad days, Meg. You don't have to be the best player. Just try hard."

Meg did want to play soccer. She could not wait until the next game. She would play hard. She would try her best even if it rained!

LOOKING BACK

SKILL PRACTICE

1. Tell about the main parts of the story. Use the story map below.

   This story is about ______________________.

   This story takes place ______________________.

   The main events are ______________________.

   The story ends when ______________________.

2. What did Meg do at home after the game?

THINK ABOUT IT

3. Tell about a time when it was important for you to try hard.

"The people in class are my friends," said Kate. "Dad, did you ever give a speech?"

"Sure," said Dad. "I give a speech almost every day. I stand in front of my class." Dad is a teacher.

"Are you ever afraid?" asked Kate.

"I used to be afraid," said Dad. "Then I learned something. I can make sure of the facts. Then I feel good about my speech."

"I'm sure of the facts," said Kate. "Did you ever give a speech, Matt?"

"I gave a speech," said Matt. "I ran for president of my school. I stood before everyone in school. I was afraid. Then I learned something. I could pretend I was not afraid. Then I wasn't afraid!"

"I can do that," said Kate. "I can pretend I'm not afraid."

Soon it was time for the speech. Kate stood in front of the class. She thought about her report. She knew all the facts. She looked at each person. They were her friends.

Then Kate began to talk. She pretended she was not afraid. She was not afraid! She talked about lions and elephants. Everyone thought her speech was great.

LOOKING BACK

SKILL PRACTICE

1. Tell about the main parts of the story. Use the story map below.

Title ______________________

Characters
Problem
Events
Solution

2. Kate looked at each person in class. Why did this make her less afraid?

THINK ABOUT IT

3. Kate asked others for help. They gave her good ideas. What are good ideas you give others?

Guide dogs go to a special school. One is called the Seeing Eye School. A dog must be fourteen months old. Then it can go to the school. First, people choose dogs to **train.** They test the dogs. Is the dog smart? Does it stay calm? A guide dog must not get scared easily. Does it obey the **trainer**? Does it follow the trainer's orders?

Each dog is trained for four months. It wears a **harness.** The trainer holds the harness. The dog walks with the trainer. It learns to cross streets. The trainer teaches the dog directions. He or she says "right" and "left." The dog learns these words. It learns in which direction to go. The trainer will often praise the dog. The dog likes praise.

◀ This guide dog is a Labrador retriever.

Soon the trainer introduces the dog to its owner. After meeting, the two work together. The dog learns to obey its owner. The owner learns how to work with the dog. Then they go home together. The owner introduces the dog to its new home. He or she shows the dog around. They go to the store together. Soon the dog knows which streets to take. It can find its way.

The owner takes good care of the dog. The dog keeps its owner safe. They become friends. They are often together for many years.

Someday you may cross a street. You may see a dog on a harness. You will see how important guide dogs are.

This owner uses his guide dog when he hikes and camps. ▶

LOOKING BACK

SKILL PRACTICE

1. This is a nonfiction article. It contains a main idea and supporting details. Show examples. Use the organizer below.

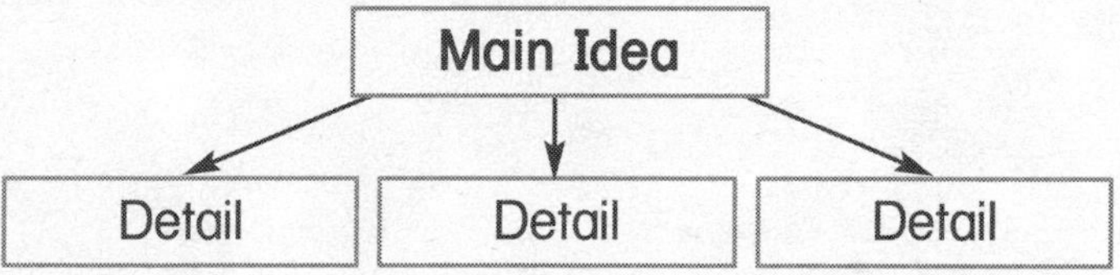

2. Dogs help in many ways. This is one main idea in the article. Tell two details that support this idea.

TALK ABOUT IT

3. What is the most important way guide dogs help people? Talk about this with a partner.

The rabbit took off on his long legs. Soon he stood at the curve in the road. He looked back. Far away he saw the turtle. He moved slowly on his short legs. The sun shone on his hard shell.

The rabbit laughed. "This will take him all day. I think I will rest. I will win the race soon enough." The rabbit lay on the grass. The sun felt warm on his ears.

The rabbit jumped up with a start. The sun was going down! He had been asleep. He looked toward the pine trees. The turtle was almost there!

The rabbit jumped up. He ran to the trees. He ran as fast as he could. But the turtle was already there. The slow turtle had won the race!

The animals had a big party. They cheered for the turtle. The wise fox said, "Sometimes the one who is slow but steady wins the race."

The Rabbit and the Turtle

LOOKING BACK

SKILL PRACTICE

1. Tell about the main parts of the story. Use the story map below.

Title ______________________

Characters
Problem
Events
Solution

2. How is the turtle different from the rabbit?

TALK ABOUT IT

3. Think of some times when "slow but steady" is better than fast. Talk about them with a partner.

The changes take time. Illustrators may work for months on one book. They want each picture to be great. Sometimes they do not like a picture. They throw it out. They start again.

At last, all the pictures are done. Then they send the pictures away. They send them to people who plan and make books.

Finally, the books are ready. The illustrators are happy. They show the book to their friends.

Illustrators have many ideas. They like to use paints and crayons to make many books that are fun to read.

Pages of books are printed on large sheets of paper. Then they are cut apart.

LOOKING BACK

SKILL PRACTICE

1. This is a nonfiction article. What is the main idea? What are some details? Use the organizer to help you.

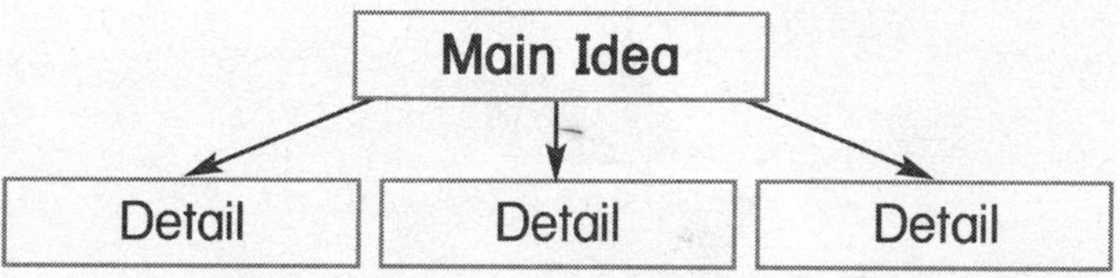

2. Why does the illustrator of a story talk to the person who wrote it?

THINK ABOUT IT

3. Before you read the article, did you guess what it would be about? Where did you find clues?

This young puffin is covered in down, or soft feathers.

Sea Gulls

Sea gulls live near the water, like penguins and puffins. Some sea gulls live near oceans. Others live near large lakes. They spend much of their time floating in the water. Sometimes sea gulls fly in the air. Sometimes they walk on the land.

Sea gulls eat almost anything. Their favorite meals are sea animals and insects. They also eat scraps of food that people leave behind.

Where do sea gulls raise their chicks? They raise them on land, like penguins and puffins. They raise them in nests. Gulls build their nests in rocky areas or wetlands. Wetlands are lands that are soaked with water. Marshes and swamps are wetlands.

A sea gull feeds its chick.

Flamingos may be red or pink.

Flamingos

Flamingos are also water birds. They live near water, like penguins and puffins and sea gulls. Flamingos are colorful birds. Their name comes from a word that means "flame." Can you guess why?

Flamingos live in large groups. Hundreds of flamingos may live in one area. Flamingos live near oceans and lakes. They also live in wetlands. Like other water birds, they eat mostly fish.

Where do flamingos raise their chicks? They raise them in nests built in the water. These nests are made of mud and shaped like cones.

Penguins, puffins, sea gulls, and flamingos all raise their chicks near water. They spend most of their time on and around water. To these birds, the water is home!

LOOKING BACK

SKILL PRACTICE

1. This is a nonfiction article. What is the main idea? Name some supporting details. Use the organizer to help you.

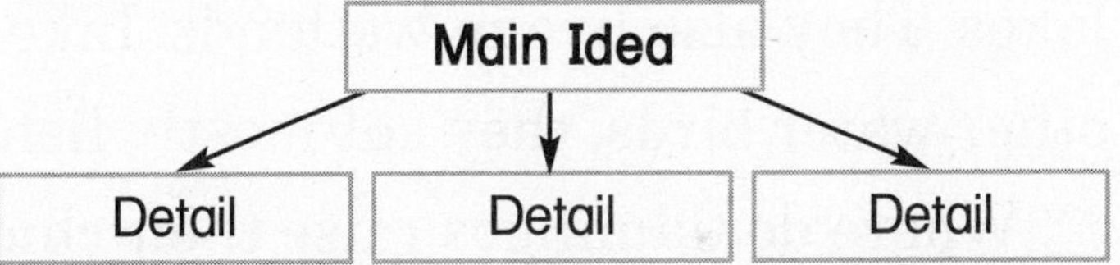

2. In what ways are penguins and flamingos alike? In what ways are they different?

TALK ABOUT IT

3. Why do you think oceans, lakes, and wetlands are home to many birds? Talk about this with a partner.

Icebergs may drift from cold to warm water. As they do, they melt. Parts may break off. The large and small pieces keep drifting in the water.

▼ Icebergs cover a large area of water near Antarctica.

Ships travel in the warmer waters. Sometimes icebergs float into their sea lanes. **Sea lanes** are where ships travel. Sailors watch for icebergs. They do not want to hit an iceberg. That could badly damage a ship.

In 1912, a ship was sailing across the Atlantic Ocean. It was called the *Titanic*. Many people were on it. Icebergs were in its sea lane. One was in the *Titanic*'s path. The ship hit the iceberg. The part of the iceberg under the water split the seams of the ship. Water poured into the ship. It sank, and many people died.

Now you know about icebergs. You know they can be dangerous. You know what the tip of an iceberg is.

So what do people mean when they say "It's just the tip of the iceberg"? They mean only a small part of something can be seen. The biggest part is hidden. That part may cause big problems!

▼ **A ship sails through icebergs near the Antarctic Peninsula.**

Tip of the Iceberg

LOOKING BACK

SKILL PRACTICE

1. This article is nonfiction. It gives details about a main idea. Use the organizer to tell the main idea and details.

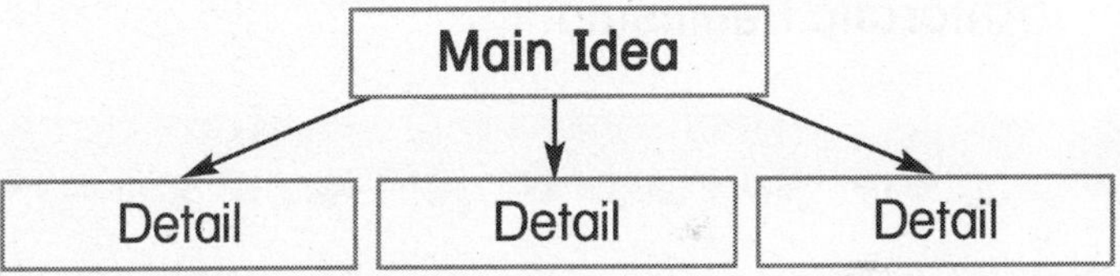

2. What could happen if an iceberg floats in a ship's sea lane?

TALK ABOUT IT

3. Draw a picture of an iceberg and a ship. Show the parts above and below water. Compare your picture with a partner's.

Tornadoes can do great damage. They can spin at up to 300 miles an hour. They can knock down trees. They can pick up cars. They can tear houses apart.

Weather forecasters watch for tornadoes. They quickly warn people about a tornado. The people need to get to safe places. They must stay there until the storm is over. Staying safe is why people must watch out for twisters.

Watch Out for Twisters!

LOOKING BACK

SKILL PRACTICE

1. This is a nonfiction article. Show examples of cause and effect in the article. Use the chart.

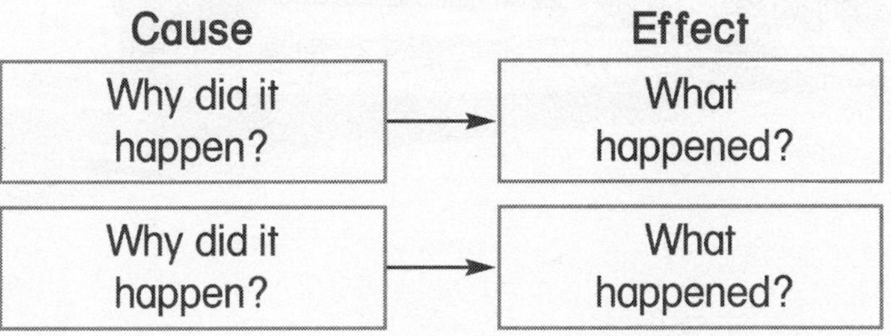

2. Think about how a tornado forms. Why do you think most tornadoes occur in spring?

TALK ABOUT IT

3. Tornadoes can be dangerous. Other storms can do damage also. Tell about a storm you saw that did damage.

"Great!" said ROCK. "I'm good with computers." Soon Eddie's homework was done.

"Tell me about TOCK," Eddie said to ROCK.

"Let me show you," ROCK answered. He pressed some computer keys.

Eddie saw TOCK. He was not bored now!

But then the computer flashed a message:

ROCK,

IT'S TIME TO COME HOME.

DAD

"I have to go," said ROCK.

"Come back soon," said Eddie. "We're friends now."

LOOKING BACK

SKILL PRACTICE

1. Tell about the main parts of the story. Use the story map.

Characters	Setting
Events	Ending

2. What did ROCK and Eddie do that was fun? Tell what they did in the order they did it.

THINK ABOUT IT

3. Do you like to read stories like "ROCK from TOCK"? Tell why or why not.

Another strange plant is a pitcher plant. Its name tells how it is shaped. Look at the pitcher plants on pages 1 and 3. Then imagine this: an insect falls into the plant and cannot climb back up the smooth sides. The insect is stuck.

A sundew plant has sticky drops on each leaf. The drops catch an insect. Then the leaf closes around it.

You can grow a sundew or a Venus flytrap at home. Then you can watch these interesting plants!

Sundew Plant ➤

LOOKING BACK

SKILL PRACTICE

1. This is a nonfiction article. It uses examples. Show how examples explain the subject. Below is part of an outline. Complete it.

I. Kinds of plants that eat insects

A.

B.

C.

2. Tell the main idea of "Plant Traps!"

THINK ABOUT IT

3. How did the examples help you understand the main idea?

▲ Sheryl and her team received the Olympic gold medal.

Some women wanted the United States to have professional teams. In 1996 they got their wish. Professional teams for women were formed. American professionals now could play in the United States. Sheryl joined a team here.

The coach talks to the team during a game.

Sheryl joined the Houston Comets. The players practiced together. They trained together. They played hard on the basketball court. Sheryl's team became national champions.

Women professionals travel to many cities. They meet a lot of fans. Playing professional basketball is hard work. But it is fun also! Sheryl Swoopes says, "It's like a dream come true."

Sheryl dribbles the ball past a teammate.

LOOKING BACK

SKILL PRACTICE

1. This is a nonfiction article. Use the organizer below to help you name the main idea and some details.

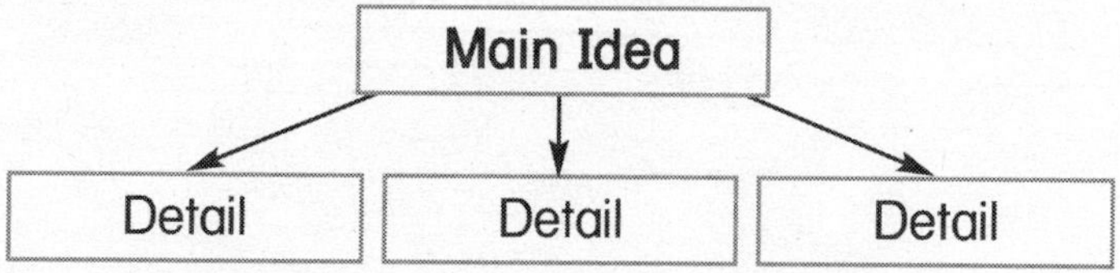

2. Sheryl Swoopes is a great woman basketball player. Name two details that support this idea.

TALK ABOUT IT

3. Why did Sheryl Swoopes say that the women's pro team was like a "dream come true"? Talk about your ideas with a partner.

JULIA: I know what we should do. Let's make plans for tomorrow. First, we will have a big breakfast.

ANNIE: *(yawns)* Yes, and after breakfast, we can go to the park. But for right now, let's turn off the light. Then we can talk all night.

JULIA: That's a good idea. We can lie down too.

Scene 3

ANNIE: *(jumps up out of the sleeping bag)* Julia, get up! We did not stay up! We fell asleep.

JULIA: *(yawns)* I guess we didn't do anything special.

ANNIE: *(looks out the window)* Look! It is morning. The sun is coming up. We can still do something special! Let's sit in the backyard. We can watch the sun rise.

Scene 4

ANNIE: *(points to the sky)* I see it! I see the sun!

JULIA: It is fun to be up early with a friend. This is special after all!

LOOKING BACK

SKILL PRACTICE

1. Tell what the play is about. Use the organizer to help you.

Characters	Setting
Events	Ending

2. Why did Annie and Julia want to stay up all night? Why didn't they stay up all night?

TALK ABOUT IT

3. Discuss with a partner what you would like to do at a sleepover. Do you and your partner have the same ideas?

In rodeos, some cowboys and cowgirls ride wild horses. Others can ride bulls. Others spin their lariats. They use them to rope calves.

The cowboys and cowgirls want to do their very best at each event. To be the best they must practice. They do the same tricks over and over again.

Maybe you will go to a rodeo with your family someday. You can cheer for the cowboys and cowgirls.

LOOKING BACK

SKILL PRACTICE

1. What is the main idea of "The Rodeo"? What are some supporting details? Use the organizer to help you answer the questions.

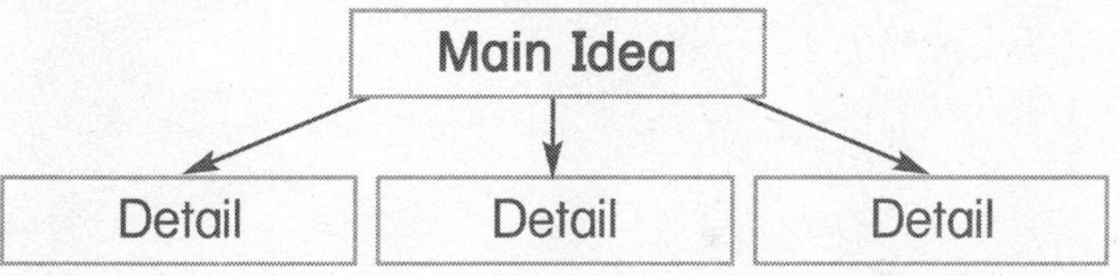

2. Why is a rodeo fun for the cowboys and cowgirls? Why is it fun for the people who watch?

THINK ABOUT IT

3. What would you most like to see at a rodeo? Tell why.

The next day, Country Mouse said, "Thanks for the good food. But city life is too exciting for me! I am going back to my home." City Mouse said good-bye. Then he went to find more fun in the city.

Country Mouse hurried back to the country.

That night he ate berries and nuts from the forest. He rested on his bed of leaves.

Country Mouse was proud of his home again. "I promise to stay here," he said.

LOOKING BACK

SKILL PRACTICE

1. Tell about the main parts of the story. Use the story map below.

Characters	Setting
Events	Ending

2. Imagine that you are the Country Mouse. Compare your home in the country to the City Mouse's home.

TALK ABOUT IT

3. Do you think the Country Mouse could ever learn to live in the city? Talk about it with a partner.

"Where will our vacation be this year?" Alex asked.

Mom saw the picture. She laughed. "That is for Aunt Pat," she said. "We will go to the beach this summer. Just as we always do."

Alex smiled. He thought. The beach is warm, not cold. There are no crowds. Alex said, "Good! I will build the biggest sand castle ever!"

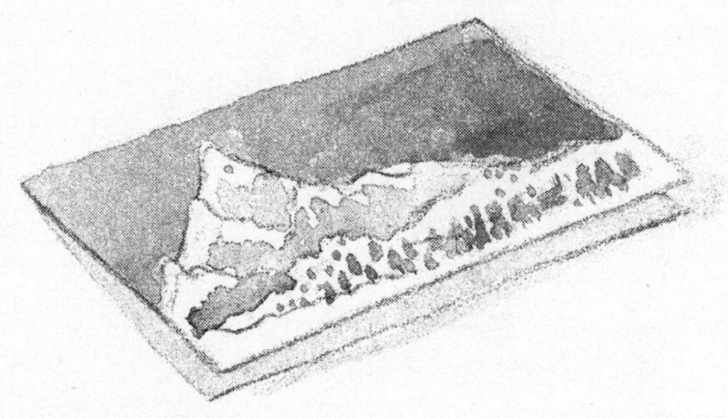

I Would Like to Visit a Fantastic Place

LOOKING BACK

SKILL PRACTICE

1. What is the story about? Use the graphic organizer to help you.

Title ______________________________

Characters
Problem
Events
Solution

2. Alex thinks of going many places. Where does he think of going first? Where is the last place he thinks of going?

THINK ABOUT IT

3. Alex thinks about different places to go on vacation. Which one would you like best? Tell why.